PRAISE FOR *DATA AND AI*

"Jordan Morrow, the godfather of data literacy, did it again! With ***Data and AI Skills*** he tackles one of the most burning questions of our time: What is the role of human beings in an age of AI-driven hyper-automation and -acceleration? Morrow's answer is the elegantly simple yet powerful formula: Data + AI + IQ + EQ = Engineered Intelligence, and it works perfectly. This is a book everyone who works with data and AI needs to read. And let's be honest—that's probably all of us."

Tiankai Feng, author of *Humanizing AI Strategy*

"Leaders need to understand that in order to get accurate data they need to empower their people to understand why they are creating data all day, every day. Jordan Morrow understands this and writes passionately about the subject in ways that non-technical folks can understand. With data in the modern world comes the inevitability of AI. AI isn't going to cure the world's ills overnight, but it isn't going away either, so we need to learn how to best utilize the power of AI for good. If you want to talk about data and AI, talk to Jordan Morrow."

Steve Taylor, Strategic Data Lead, National Fire Chiefs Council, UK

"While most data and AI books focus on tools, models, and technical capability, this book boldly puts people at the centre. It's about rewiring how we think, how we learn, and how we work. Jordan Morrow keeps you engaged and curious throughout, showing how personalization and human-centric design help individuals and organizations meet people where they are, build genuine confidence, make better decisions, strengthen collaboration, and solve real-world problems—without the burnout."

Rosanne Werner, CEO, XcelerateIQ

"It's not often you encounter someone with Jordan Morrow's depth of technical expertise and global reputation who is equally committed to bringing others along on the journey. He has that rare gift of translating the most abstract data and AI concepts into clear, relatable, and thought-provoking actions—and he brings the same clarity to his writing: direct, jargon-free, and grounded in real-world experience."

Simone Pozniak, Head: Data and Analytics, Webber Wentzel

"Jordan Morrow's ***Data and AI Skills*** cuts through the hype and delivers concrete guidance for professionals who need to understand and leverage AI responsibly. It's a practical reference for building both the skills and the judgment to make AI work in real-world contexts."

Cecilia Dones, Founder and Chief Data Officer, 3 Standard Deviations

Data and AI Skills

Gain the Confidence You Need to Succeed

Jordan Morrow

First published in Great Britain and the United States in 2026 by Kogan Page Limited

Kogan Page
Kogan Page Ltd, 2nd Floor, 45 Gee Street, London EC1V 3RS, United Kingdom
Kogan Page Inc, 8 W 38th Street, Suite 902, New York, NY 10018, USA
www.koganpage.com

EU Representative (GPSR)
Authorised Rep Compliance Ltd, Ground Floor, 71 Baggot Street Lower, Dublin D02 P593, Ireland
www.arccompliance.com

Kogan Page books are printed on paper from sustainable forests.

ISBNs

Hardback 978 1 3986 2415 3
Paperback 978 1 3986 2413 9
Ebook 978 1 3986 2414 6

British Library Cataloguing-in-Publication Data
A CIP record for this book is available from the British Library.

Library of Congress Cataloging-in-Publication Data
A CIP record for this book is available from the Library of Congress

Typeset by Integra Software Services, Pondicherry
Printed and bound by CPI Group (UK) Ltd, Croydon CR0 4YY

This book is dedicated to my wife, Cari Lyn, and my five kids. I also dedicate this book to my puppy, who is my morning partner, sitting by me as I journal or read, or who is with me on a morning drive.

Finally, I dedicate this book to my late mother, who passed away in 2025, the year I finished this manuscript. She was a wonderful grandmother and called me her knight in shining armor in her last days. Love you, Mom!

CONTENTS

PART TWO
The Human Factor

ABOUT THE AUTHOR

Jordan Morrow is known as the "Godfather of Data Literacy," having helped to pioneer the field, and travelling the world speaking about the topic, including to organizations such as Nike, Fidelity Investments, BMW, and the United Nations. Jordan is the founder of Bodhi Data and has held multiple leadership positions at different organizations.

Apart from his work in data and AI, Jordan spends his time with his family and doing things he enjoys. His favorite sport is rugby and he is a rugby coach at the University of Utah. Jordan also enjoys fitness, reading, and journaling. He is the author of *Be Data Literate*, *Be Data Driven*, *Be Data Analytical*, and *Business 101 for the Data Professional*, all published by Kogan Page.

ACKNOWLEDGMENTS

There are probably so many people to thank that I may forget some, so I will acknowledge all those that have helped to support me in my career, not only with speaking opportunities but also in my writing and for buying my books. I have also had support to help me build the world of data literacy and I acknowledge all those who have helped me in my data literacy work.

Introduction

Data and AI Confidence

Fear, hope, anxiety, excitement, overwhelm. There is a myriad of feelings that people may have toward AI in the world today. Some may fear that it will take their jobs, whereas others may feel it will enhance them. Some may hope that it can help to improve business processes, and some may be fearful that the wrong incentives are in place. Some may just feel overwhelmed or have no idea what is going on, and some may be jumping feet first into learning, growing, and developing AI skills.

Overall, our feelings are important considerations and shouldn't be taken lightly. In fact, *Scientific American* says that it is logical to feel anxious around artificial intelligence,[1] but the way we approach AI matters to find our place at the table and figure out what we want to do with this technology. How can you approach AI in an empowering way? What skills can you learn to succeed? What mindset should you adopt for success? What are the key skills that will empower you? These are all questions that will be answered throughout this book to inspire more data and AI confidence.

Negative feelings around AI aren't unfounded, as talk of layoffs or actual layoffs occur around us. We see the job market can fluctuate. We work toward success, but at times feel like we aren't getting anywhere, or we may ask ourselves: "What is the use?"

As I write this Introduction in 2025, we are seeing much hype around AI and its capabilities, but how much true return on investment (ROI) is happening on a large scale? We may hear it is here to take all the jobs, or we may hear a positive soundbite that AI is going to solve all our problems. Ask yourself this question: are you using AI in some capacity? This could be using a generative AI model to help you brainstorm ideas, or maybe your company has implemented machine learning to automate time-consuming tasks. You may have heard that AI is going to do this, or technology is going to do that. I hope you are embracing this revolution.

Although AI seems very new, it is important to know that we have had it for a while. The term artificial intelligence goes back to 1956 when John McCarthy coined the term.[2] It has been on its own journey, advancing over time. So, it is not necessarily new to the world, but something shifted on 30 November 2022. This date marked when ChatGPT, OpenAI's chatbot, became accessible to the public, which launched a revolution and rapid change. From newer terms such as "generative AI" or "AI agents" to older, more established expressions like "machine learning" and "natural language processing" recirculating in discussion, people and businesses have had to adapt. AI is not a new concept, but for all of us, our skills and development matter. Here are some metrics that can help us realize how big this market will be by 2030:

- The market size is set to reach $1.339 billion
- AI will have an estimated 21 percent net increase on the United States GDP.[3]

For individuals, the key is finding how you fit into this evolution and revolution. Do you want to gain more technical AI skills? Do you want to learn how to prompt better? Do you want to progress into a leadership role? Do you know how to thrive in a data driven or AI driven organization? There are many spots you can fit in.

Now, one may ask the question: what does the future look like with AI? However, I am not sure anyone knows. Could we see AGI (artificial general intelligence) or ASI (artificial superintelligence)? Maybe. Do we see the advent of consumable quantum computing? Maybe. Overall, let's not focus on the technological aspect because, ultimately, in-depth knowledge about a specific technology could become irrelevant or even obsolete. Instead, we should focus on the skills aspect, which can help us to be adaptable, problem-solve, find solutions, and achieve greater success with AI, regardless of how the future takes shape. Let's focus on the right mindset to keep on forging ahead with AI, to learn about it, integrate it in our lives, and adopt it.

Right now, with all going on around us in the world of AI, becoming more data and AI literate will provide more confidence, and having the right mindset toward these topics can help one be more successful. Learning new skills, bringing forward creativity, and learning how to be augmented instead of superseded by the AI can help empower our confidence toward success.

In this book, one central idea that we will explore is a new formula:

Data + AI + IQ + EQ = Engineered Intelligence

As you can see, there are four parts to the formula: data, AI (artificial intelligence), IQ (human intelligence), and EQ (emotional intelligence). The data and AI impart information, insight, and intelligence to us, which we may not have. The human skills of IQ and EQ combined with data and AI enable us to use the information to empower a decision or outcome, resulting in Engineered Intelligence. Therefore, Engineered Intelligence is a culmination of these four parts, which can be used to drive more successful outcomes from our decisions. Skills in each of these areas can be developed, so an individual can move themselves away from fear and anxiety and into confidence and assurance. Imagine your career being enhanced and empowered through data and AI, such as the time in your job being freed up to do projects or creative, more strategic tasks.

We will cover lots in this book, including what data and AI confidence looks like, the definitions of data and AI literacy and how they can be applied, and the importance of human factors (IQ and EQ). Within AI, the human elements matter greatly. You bring experience, ideas, and thoughts that give essential context to any data or AI driven decision. We will also explore building better value from data and AI. Finally, we will explore mindset and apply it to the formula included in this Introduction.

All of these topics we'll cover are relevant whether you are starting your data and AI journey completely fresh or want to continue to increase your confidence, so jump in. Remember, you have a place at the data and AI table: start building your skills and/or bringing them more to life.

Key Terminology

Before moving onto the rest of the book, you may want to familiarize yourself with the following terms. Now, please do not think that you have to memorize all of this before you go on—and please note that this doesn't include all the possible terms you could learn. However, familiarizing yourself with terminology and how these terms apply to data and AI work can help you develop confidence and skills. Did you ever ask yourself in math class growing up: "Where will I ever use this in real life?" By understanding terminology, by understanding the applicability of terms and concepts, you can see where they will be used in real life.

Data Terms

Data—Let's look at data as information to enable us to make decisions based on reason.

Database—If data is information, a database is a store of all of this information.

Data warehouse—This is a system used for reporting and data analysis and is a central component of business intelligence.[4] This system can represent data in a dashboard, for example. Data warehouses are a key part of data storytelling because visualizing the data is an important step for this.

Data science—Think of data science as a more advanced analysis and experimentation with data. A significant area of data science is statistics.

Data visualization—This is where data is displayed in certain ways, such as in charts, instead of reading row after row of data insights, so that insights can be observed more easily.

Data analysis—Essentially, data analysis is a method to inspect, clean, transform, and model data to discover insights and information. This can be done with many techniques and different types of data.[5]

Analytics—Analytics is about finding patterns within the data. It helps to turn information into insights, using statistics, programming, and research.[6]

Descriptive analytics—There are four levels of analytics, and the first level is descriptive. Think about it as the "what" level. Imagine you go to a doctor, and they tell you that you are sick—this is descriptive.

Diagnostic analytics—This is the second level of analytics; the insight level. It is the "why" behind the "what is happening." Going back to our doctor example: the doctor says you're sick and details the specific issue.

Predictive analytics—This is the third level of analytics. Going back to our doctor, they can say you are sick, here is why, and I predict if you do this, i.e., take specific medicine, you can get better.

Prescriptive analytics—This is the fourth and final level of analytics. Here, this is where the machines can tell us what to do. Like a doctor giving us a prescription, it is an external thing to help us get better. Think of this like a machine offering the business external guidance.

Data literacy—The ability to read, work with, analyze, and communicate with data.[7] While the majority of people aren't going to be data scientists, data literacy ensures that they are empowered and confident.

Coding—Coding is writing instructions for computers and other hardware.[8]

SQL (Structured Query Language)—Pronounced "sequel," this is a common coding language that was developed by IBM. It allows users to do tasks such as querying data, creating and modifying database structures, and managing access permissions[9]

Python—Python is a more advanced coding language and is a very popular coding language for data scientists.

Data storytelling—This is a powerful skill where a narrative is crafted, which is supported by data points. This narrative can be used to help drive decisions, persuade audiences, or for a business purpose.

Data governance—Data governance is managing the data, focusing on its quality, security, and availability.

Data strategy—A data strategy is simply how an organization is going to use data to achieve its goals and objectives.

Chief Data Officer (CDO)—This is a leader in the organization's data space, most likely leading the organization's data work and strategy.

AI Terms

Artificial intelligence (AI)—AI is a collective term for computer systems that are capable of performing complex tasks that have historically been done by humans.

Machine learning (ML)—Machine learning is where a system learns from data and this learning can then apply to future data.

Algorithm—An algorithm is a procedure that is used for solving problems or performing operations in mathematics, computer programming, and computing science.[10]

Generative AI—Generative AI, also called GenAI, is a type of AI that has the ability to create text, images, video, and more. It relies on sophisticated machine learning models and identifies patterns and relationships and encodes them.[11]

Natural language processing (NLP)—This is a subfield of computer science and AI that enables computers to understand and communicate with human language.[12]

Neural network—A neural network is a type of computing architecture that is based on how our human brains function. They are used in machine learning for deep learning.[13]

Generative machine learning—Generative machine learning is similar to generative AI but instead, it is generating machine learning itself and not content like generative AI.

Prompt—This is how we ask questions of generative AI. The better we are at prompting, the better the response generative AI will give us.

Prompt engineering—Prompt engineering is the process of improving our prompts for better results. We want to iterate and improve our prompts as we are using AI to drive better results.

Vibe coding—Vibe coding is about making the coding experience more fun, interactive, and enjoyable. This takes it away from more traditional, rigid structures associated with coding.[14]

Hallucinations—These are model outputs that are either nonsensical or outright false.[15] This can be a bad thing if you aren't evaluating and working through the output to understand if it is valid or not.

AI literacy—In this book, AI literacy is the ability to prompt AI, evaluate the prompt response, and execute decisions.

Jumping In

Now that you have some terminology, I want you to do something for me as you read this book. I want you to take notes, write things down. You may come across frameworks in this book that can help you to be more successful with data and AI, that can help you develop more confidence. Don't just take these frameworks at face value. Instead, find ways to customize them toward your personal goals. There may be things I suggest in a framework that won't resonate with you, and you need to change them. Don't hesitate. Jump in and learn what does and doesn't work for you. Make these things your own.

I am big on writing and journaling in my life. We may think to ourselves: "I will remember this later," but what happens when later comes? We don't always remember it. Sometimes, I walk to someplace in my house and forget what I was going there for. Does that ever happen to you? So, write things down. Experiment and write down what did and didn't work for you. Write down your ideas. Write down things that you hear from someone that may have inspired you. Take notes on things that happened and didn't happen. Celebrate your wins and find success in your journey.

You have a seat at the data and AI table; don't forget that. As you sit down, it may seem intimidating, it may seem difficult, it may seem overwhelming, but as you would find on a long journey, the first step may be the hardest you take. Take the step anyway. As you go through this book, find what that seat looks like for you, sit down, and enjoy the work. Don't let fear override you. Allow your IQ and EQ to take part in this data and AI world we live in.

Notes

1 L. Leffer. "AI Anxiety" Is on the Rise—Here's How to Manage It, *Scientific American*, October 2, 2023, www.scientificamerican.com/article/ai-anxiety-is-on-the-rise-heres-how-to-manage-it/ (archived at https://perma.cc/A89K-E8XP)

2 S. Pradhan. Who Coined the Term Artificial Intelligence: Know the History, Analytics Insight, October 17, 2024, www.analyticsinsight.net/artificial-intelligence/who-coined-the-term-artificial-intelligence-know-the-history (archived at https://perma.cc/R73H-5FA5)

3 K. Haan and L. Holznienkemper. 22 Top AI Statistics And Trends, *Forbes*, October 16, 2024, www.forbes.com/advisor/business/ai-statistics/d (archived at https://perma.cc/YVU7-J2ZX)

4 Wikipedia. Data Warehouse, en.wikipedia.org/wiki/Data_warehouse (archived at https://perma.cc/R8NJ-7H35)

5 M. Crabtree and A. Nehme. What Is Data Analysis? An Expert Guide with Examples, DataCamp, November 10, 2024, www.datacamp.com/blog/what-is-data-analysis-expert-guide (archived at https://perma.cc/6Q8Q-PUZP)

6 M. Webb. Analytics, Techopedia, November 18, 2024, www.techopedia.com/definition/analytics (archived at https://perma.cc/EX8L-SLSW)

7 Qlik. Data Literacy, www.qlik.com/us/data-literacy (archived at https://perma.cc/SD2K-PM76)

8 A. Nduta. What Is Coding? A Beginner's Guide, CareerFoundry, January 10, 2023, careerfoundry.com/en/blog/web-development/what-is-coding/ (archived at https://perma.cc/E9WR-CX7D)

9 GeeksforGeeks. What Is SQL? August 23, 2025, www.geeksforgeeks.org/what-is-sql/ (archived at https://perma.cc/8FQ9-CKLS)

10 A. Gillis. What Is an Algorithm? TechTarget, July 29, 2024, www.techtarget.com/whatis/definition/algorithm (archived at https://perma.cc/8UMK-NMWD)

11 M. Scapicchio and C Stryker. What Is Generative AI?, IBM, March 22, 2024, www.ibm.com/think/topics/generative-ai (archived at https://perma.cc/9ZPU-PPHF)

12 J. Holdsworth and C Stryker. What Is NLP (Natural Language Processing)?, IBM, August 11, 2024, www.ibm.com/think/topics/natural-language-processing (archived at https://perma.cc/23Z5-KSF6)

13 Cloudflare. What Is a Neural Network? www.cloudflare.com/learning/ai/what-is-neural-network/ (archived at https://perma.cc/LLY4-DAPS)

14 GeeksforGeeks. What Is Vibe Coding, September 8, 2025, www.geeksforgeeks.org/techtips/what-is-vibe-coding/ (archived at https://perma.cc/6VEW-737K)

15 Telus Digital. Generative AI Hallucinations: Why They Occur and How to Prevent Them, June 20, 2024, www.telusdigital.com/insights/ai-data/article/generative-ai-hallucinations (archived at https://perma.cc/X9NF-HA2U)

PART ONE

Data and AI

1

The Formula for Success in the Age of Data and AI

In the Introduction, I introduced you to my new formula. Have you memorized it yet? Don't feel bad if you haven't, as this chapter is going to recap it and help you understand it better. Knowledge is power and as you develop knowledge around the formula, I hope you take notes and find your seat at the table. Make it a comfy one because as you feast at the table, you can find data and AI augmenting your skills and knowledge in ways you may not have known could happen. The key isn't the memorization of the formula, although that may help you out, but it is important to understand how this formula can become a part of how you use data and AI in your career.

Here it is again:

Data + AI + IQ + EQ = Engineered Intelligence

Notice it is two parts human and two parts technology (or non-human). Like having the right ingredients for a cookie recipe, this formula provides the right ingredients for success with data and AI. One great thing is that each of us is unique, and we may never find two people that make the same cookie. Also, we want to make sure we know that the recipe is not equal parts everything. Sometimes, in a recipe there is more of one ingredient than another. In our formula, one part may outweigh another part, and that is okay. It is figuring out that for each end product the recipe is building, in our case Engineered Intelligence, we are learning to break down the ingredients for success.

Let's help all embrace this formula, using our human and emotional intelligence with technology to create successes in each of our unique roles. Can you think of a "cookie recipe" in business? Things that would resemble putting things into the proper order to ensure you get success? Well, that may be a lot of the processes you have in your career, such as building a new product or operations for a client. Ensure you understand the different pieces of the formula for success. You wouldn't add salt instead of sugar in a cookie recipe, as this wouldn't be tasty. In fact, it will ruin the cookies to not have one of the ingredients in them. Data, AI, IQ, and EQ are all essential "ingredients" that cannot be forgotten if you desire maximum success.

A Forbes article, titled "The Dark Side of AI: Tracking the Decline of Human Cognitive Skills," talks about how AI is reshaping the way we think, as AI is "thinking" for us.[1] This highlights the need to remember the human element of the formula, human intelligence and emotional intelligence, which should be augmented by AI and not forgotten. Our brains have the ability to lose critical thinking skills, and it looks like it is happening, according to *Psychology Today*.[2] AI makes it easier for us not to have to think deeply because it gives us answers immediately, without the need for extensive research, and we can just use those answers. Therefore, there is a risk that we may become spectators to the decision making in our lives. When we don't have to think, then that cognitive muscle may weaken.

Early in your career, think of your ability to problem-solve and to critically think as a muscle. When we work out and use our muscles, they can grow stronger. What happens when we stop working out? Our muscles can atrophy. Let's do the same with our problem solving and critical thinking "muscles." Work them, and they won't decline. Think of the reality of using AI too much in your career: inadvertently you may lose sight of the fact that you are using it too much and not realize you are missing out on using key pieces of your mind. Don't let this happen to you. Dig in and succeed with both data and AI, and yourself, the human.

Now, with each of us being unique we can understand that each of us has a place in each part of this formula. Yes, even if you don't work with data in some form (like as an analyst or scientist), you have a spot within the data world. Even if you don't work in AI but use it, you have a spot within the AI world. It is up to us to determine what that place is and how you approach it. We all can develop confidence in data and AI, but you need to remember that I can write these words, but it won't mean much if you don't apply them. One strategy I recommend is to take notes, writing your thoughts and ideas about how the content in this book applies to you. Look for ways to apply yourself in each area so you can build skills and work toward your data and AI confidence. Then, set goals and time to experiment and move forward with the areas. Don't just read: read to learn, apply, and develop.

Here in the first chapter, we will go through the formula itself and explore its four elements. We will also discuss how each person, no matter their role in an organization, has a seat at the table and look at a few examples of how we can encourage this confidence in a business setting. But to begin, let's give a brief history of data and AI, and how we arrived where we are today.

Data and AI: A Brief History

I mentioned in the Introduction that the term "AI" was coined all the way back in 1956, and the idea of data potentially spans back thousands of years to when someone was trying to figure out which berry was good to eat, and which one wasn't. Maybe we collected data on which animal would eat us, and which one wouldn't. But here we are today, and data science is everywhere, and it feels like everyone is discussing AI. Let's build some foundational knowledge of the data and AI spaces to help you on your journey.

AI History

Artificial intelligence is where we are able to simulate human intelligence in the form of a machine. Think about the different skills we as humans possess when it comes to our intelligence and then picture computers or technology with the ability to carry out tasks that we normally do ourselves. So far, though, as of the writing of this book, AI is not necessarily able to truly be compassionate or have emotions. While it may simulate these, AI has not achieved the human level of intelligence in some cases.

AI, like all other technologies, has advanced greatly from its emergence in the 1950s:[3]

- The **1950s and 1960s** can be seen as the foundational years of AI. In 1950 the great Alan Turing published his landmark paper "Computing Machinery and Intelligence." We will speak about the Turing Test later in this chapter. But an understanding that AI has been around for a while and yet we all still have jobs today can drive optimism in our lives, considering we don't want to feel like the AI is going to supersede us all together.
- The **1960s to 1980s** can be seen as an expansion era. During this time, we saw early natural language processing, the world's first mobile robot, and the establishment of AI institutions. It was in the 60s that the first chatbot was built.
- In the **1980s and 1990s** AI development was quieter, also known as an AI winter, due to waning funding and the fact that the computing power needed to truly bring about AI success wasn't there. AI was waiting for our computers to catch up.
- From **2000 to 2019**, we saw some steady growth in AI. This steady growth could be seen in the advancing of AI in neural networks or deep learning.
- Since **2020** we have seen an explosive rise in AI. In 2023, OpenAI's Large Language Model ChatGPT became public. One thing this new AI did that the others didn't was to make AI more consumable. How many of you knowingly used AI before ChatGPT launched widely? You may have encountered it without knowing that's what you were using. But now, we can be very aware that what we are using is AI, and that is great. Embrace it and upskill yourself to be able to have a greater understanding of AI, to empower you to have more success with this technology.

Overall, AI's growth has caused much human excitement. However, excitement doesn't always translate directly to real success. Sometimes, it goes in the complete opposite direction. Think back to the dotcom bubble. There were many online businesses trying to be a valuable company, but without true foundational power and success. When this occurred, in the end, companies that were seen to be very valuable but had no true foundation went bust. The best approach to take is to be tempered, study things and learn, and work through use cases to empower ourselves and our organizations with AI success.

The Turing Test

Now, let's discuss the Turing Test. The Turing Test was created by Alan Turing, a British mathematician and logician. His test basically checks whether a machine demonstrates the same intelligence as a human. When a human and a computer are asked the same question, if you cannot tell which response is the human and which is the computer, the Turing Test is passed. Think about the work with AI today: AI can write great emails or give good responses, and we may not be able to tell which is a human and which is a machine. However, what about when the same AI tool gives a result and it doesn't feel very human? Does it sound too smart? Too technical? Does it need to change its tone for the user? While you use AI, for example prompting ChatGPT or Gemini to answer a question, use your critical thinking skills and your IQ and EQ. Ask yourself: can I tell if this response is AI generated, or does it sound like a human?

AI is powerful and the fact it can give us good responses or outcomes is something we should utilize in our roles, where appropriate, but we should always have the Turing Test in mind. We should also be evaluating the responses to make sure they add up and make sense. Don't just grab an AI response and assume it's fine. Evaluate it and make sure it is valid. If you don't know whether that AI response is a good one, ask it for sources and ensure the sources are real. Don't just use information the AI gave you without checking it. This may get you in a bit of trouble. Use cases are also a good way to ensure we are using AI in a helpful manner, and we will discuss these in Chapter 6.

Now, we shouldn't view the world of AI as just another technology or tool but something more. AI can be our partner, helping us to generate ideas. We now live in an era where AI is evolving rapidly, so our ability to deal with it effectively matters. Our ability to adopt it and adapt to new technologies will be key to our future success.

In the world of data and analytics, I have my three Cs: curiosity, creativity, and critical thinking. All three of these concepts are not technical in nature and by using them, we can develop more confidence in our ability to use data. As you can see, one of my three Cs of data literacy is critical thinking. Why do you think critical thinking matters in the world of data and AI? Well, we want to ensure the data and AI are accurate, for one, but we need to ensure we apply our human element to the data and AI. We don't want to just rely on it and not understand if it is positioned and answered correctly, or even true. If we are too reliant on AI, will we lose our critical thinking muscle? We will explore this later in this chapter and discuss it later in the book too. Let's now look at the history of data.

Data History

Data has been around for centuries. We have been collecting data, using data, and making decisions with data, so hopefully everyone realizes they have the ability to be data literate. People may use data more than they know, but they need to develop their data confidence because now, in our day and age, there is a lot of data. Just how much data? As of July 2025, the world generated 2.5 quintillion bytes of data each day.[4] How many zeros are in a quintillion? 18. That is 2.5 with 18 zeros after it! Therefore, one may feel overwhelmed with all the data in front of them and being asked to do something with it. Remember, not everyone needs to be a data analyst or data scientist, but they should be confident and comfortable with data. Although you may not realize it, we all use data to do things, like information about flying somewhere for our holiday, or looking at a gas gauge for a vehicle or a weather app when traveling. These are data points we may use for decisions.

Writing a history of data is more challenging because what we classify as data may not have been the same years ago; we may have been using data, even if we didn't call it that. So, let's give an approximate breakdown of data history:[5]

- If we go back to **19,000 BCE**, we can find that our Paleolithic ancestors used a tool called the Ishango Bone to perform simple calculations.
- Back in the **1640s**, death information was collected by John Graunt, who became known as the "Father of Modern Statistics."[6]
- In the **1880s**, the era of processing data was born with punch cards for train tickets.
- In **1928** we saw the concept of data storage taking shape. This has a big part to play within the world of data science, as the data stored can be used for data driven decision making and data science applications.
- In more recent times and **the present day**, the era of data science has emerged: databases (although this may include data from long ago), data literacy, big data, and data governance. There are multiple areas in the data space and for us, what matters is that we are intelligently using data and not just jumping on buzzword bandwagons.

Like AI, the world of data has also been surrounded by a lot of hype, but buzzwords and new terminology can plague and obfuscate the realities of both data and AI and how they should be used. Think of terms like "big data," "data science," or even the field close to me, "data literacy." Each of these may have seemed like a solution to it all, but hype alone doesn't solve business problems. Instead, we need to consider the human elements of our formula again, to find value and solutions.

With a brief history of data covered, how can we view this world of data and AI in a practical way to help bring success? Part of what we can do is take on our own accountability and responsibility to develop skills in these spaces. Don't fear the future; approach it with optimism, developing skills that will help you with data and AI and improve your confidence.

The Formula

Let's dive into the formula to explain how it can provide success for us with regard to data and AI:

Data + AI + IQ + EQ = Engineered Intelligence

From a definition perspective, this formula means: when one combines a solid understanding and literacy within data and AI and uses this to help make a decision, with the addition of our human intelligence (IQ) and emotional intelligence (EQ), we create Engineered Intelligence. Now, Engineered Intelligence is intelligence that can empower us toward more successful outcomes, objectives, and decisions. As you find your place in this data and AI era, you can experience more success with Engineered Intelligence and your seat at the table can be more comfortable. This is great. Each of us has that seat and using the formula, you can find what your seat looks like.

These elements of the formula hopefully help you face the future with less fear or anxiety and transform these feelings to optimism. By developing more knowledge and understanding, we are empowered to thrive instead of jumping out of a plane with a potentially faulty parachute. Empower yourself instead of lacking understanding for success. One key watchout is to not forget we may have blind spots in our IQ and EQ. While we want to ensure we use our IQ and EQ, we also need to ensure we acknowledge the blind spots and work toward filling them in. Also know that it is okay to have these blind spots. Instead of worrying about them, put plans in place to empower you and help you succeed.

You should apply this formula and develop personal accountability toward your own development, instead of hoping and wishing for success—or for AI to go away! One should not watch the current revolution taking place go by. Embrace it and then push forward with it. Below, we will look at each space individually and then you can learn more about where you fit in with the formula.

Data

The data space is one full of different roles, positions, and terms: data analyst, data architect, data engineer, data governance, data management, Chief Data Officer, Chief Analytics Officer, data visualization, data literacy, data consumer.

Data is the backbone for a lot of the work done in AI and in data driven decision making. Within AI, data is what AI can learn from, whether it is quantitative (numerical) or qualitative (text) data. Then, the AI can deliver data driven prompt responses, which enable us to make decisions that are likely to be more successful. A personal example from my life will show how data played a key role in a required decision. I was driving home from a rugby session, and my tire gauge eventually showed the tire was down to 0 air pressure. Not good. I pulled off the freeway and got the car towed. After new tires were put on the car, I was driving again and a different tire was showing low PSI. I filled it up and it appeared to be okay. How does this relate to data? Well, you may not think of it as data, but when the information showed the pressure was 0, I saw that data point in front of me and I could then make a decision. Thankfully, I followed the data point, so I didn't ruin part of my car.

In the AI world, while AI can seem powerful or work really well, it is predicated on this world of data. When AI learns, it is learning from data. When we prompt a generative AI tool and like the result, that AI tool has been built off data. One key thing to do is ensure the data feeding the AI model is good, strong data so our results from the AI are also strong and good.

Data is all around us. Gas prices, home and food prices, temperatures, sports data. There are different data points available to us and even simple data points can lead to effective decision making. Now think about the massive amounts of data that organizations are obtaining right now. What are they doing with it? What kind of AI is the data training? How do individuals fit in with the data?

Data is a backbone for organizations, and all employees use it on a day-to-day basis. Within data, I have what I call my four rights of data (sometimes I call it the four rights of data and AI). These are:

- the RIGHT data
- at the RIGHT time
- for the RIGHT objective
- with the RIGHT literacy

Essentially, data should be accessible and at our fingertips for us to succeed with our formula. But we need those skills to understand it, know what it means, be able to interpret it, and how we can communicate and succeed with it. We will cover this more in Chapter 3 about data literacy.

These four rights of data help us not to feel overwhelmed by the large amounts of data that is at our fingertips, or the fact that AI is available to us. The four rights help to break things down in an effective manner.

When we have the objective we are looking to achieve, we can then get the "right data." Then, we want to ensure we have it at the "right time." Then, we ensure we are using the data and work toward the objective correctly. Finally, we can learn and ensure we have the right skills, or literacy, to actually use the data and AI. If we don't have those skills or have the data at the right time, we may miss. So, these four rights of data (and they can be used with AI, too) can help us not to be overwhelmed and use a targeted approach going forward.

Artificial Intelligence (AI)

Does the term "artificial intelligence" term scare you? Intimidate you? Excite you? Don't have a clue what it means? Don't worry, you don't need to know all the ins and outs. When we think about AI, what I want you to do is understand it, how to use it, how to evaluate it, and how to make decisions with it. This is essentially a definition for AI literacy, which we will explore later in the book. AI is a powerful feature in our lives when we use it as our partner. AI has different faces it can take on: generative AI like a ChatGPT or Gemini, which can help us with productivity, create ideas, write for us, using machine learning and predictive modeling.

IQ (Human Intelligence or Intelligence Quotient)

The world of human intelligence is so important in our formula. There is a fear surrounding discussions around AI that people will be left behind by the AI revolution, but AI should be a partner, not something to supersede us. Therefore, our human intelligence needs to be in place.

Another reason it matters in our formula is I want all of our personal ideas, experiences, and intuition to be a part of the equation. I don't want you to think that your gut feel or your ideas aren't welcome. They are! Instead, view the AI and data as offering support. Sometimes your gut feel and intuition need to take charge, and sometimes the data and AI do. But, as we grow and drive through data and AI work, you will better understand where human context is required. Plus, my three Cs of data literacy, curiosity, creativity, and critical thinking, should be a part of the overall world you adopt with data and AI. There is more to come on IQ in Chapter 7 and Chapter 8.

Overall, each of us has intelligence that can be utilized in the world of data and AI. Don't miss out: be curious and ask "do I have any knowledge that I can use on this?" or "do I have personal data points that the data and/or AI response is missing? Do I have knowledge that people aren't seeing that will help this decision?" Don't fear speaking up. Speak up, share your ideas, share your thoughts.

EQ (Emotional Intelligence or Emotional Quotient)

The final piece of the formula is emotional intelligence, which is covered in detail in Chapter 7 and Chapter 8 alongside human intelligence. Emotional intelligence is the ability to understand our own emotions and the emotions of others,[7] and can help in the deployment and management of data and AI. Having self-awareness and awareness of what others are thinking and feeling toward AI and data are essential skills. A lot of data and AI work is people work. Managing stress and uncertainty, as well as helping people to understand their rightful place in this world of data and AI, can help them to develop the right mindset for success. Mindset is covered in Chapter 12.

The Dunning-Kruger effect, a cognitive bias where people wrongly overestimate their abilities in a specific subject,[8] is worth drawing attention to. AI is a gamechanger, and its evolution could cause some displacement. That said, recognizing we don't know what we don't know can be good for us. Controlling our own emotions and helping others with theirs in the AI space is a key way to help drive more success with AI.

Success—Engineered Intelligence

What does success look like at the end of our formula Data + AI + IQ + EQ = Engineered Intelligence? Success can mean delivering answers to questions, empowering decisions, finding more value in your decisions, helping to innovate or create, or delivering outcomes. Why do we use data and AI? One reason is to empower decisions. Ask yourself: what would success look like to you when it comes to data and AI use in your career? How can you ensure that your IQ and EQ helps you with data and AI?

Ultimately, one way we can describe success is that you are now more confident in how you can use the four pieces of the formula to empower yourself. That can mean simply using data to make small decisions, like asking a weather app what to pack for a business trip, or utilizing AI to help you design a strategy and roadmap for your business and then applying it. Overall, data and AI do not have to represent a monumental thing, like climbing Mount Everest. Eventually, maybe you do tackle that climb, but you can take small steps to utilizing data and AI more in your life before making a big breakthrough.

A Seat at the Table

Why would I say everyone has a seat at the table of data and AI? Is that really true? The answer is yes! It may be too often that people feel they didn't go to school to study a subject, so they don't have a seat at the table. That is just not true. What if you went to school for arts or literature? Wonderful, bring yourself to the table. What if you started a career in plumbing or as an electrician? That's great, come to the table. But what does this mean?

Having a seat at the table can be thought of as like having a big meal. The big meal can consist of different things where people have different tastes, ideas, conversations, and so forth. With data and AI, there shouldn't be any empty chairs at the table. Everyone has human intelligence that can be a part of the conversation. What if this person or that person brings an idea or thought that helps an AI be prompted in a more effective way? What if someone has experience that empowers them to look at a solution differently and then it can be applied to AI? What if someone is good at critical thinking and asking questions, so they turn those questions over to the more technical people? You don't have to have a technical background to sit at the table. There are seats at the table that are open for all to enjoy, and I hope people embrace data and AI in this way.

So how do you sit at the table yourself, and how can we be more inclusive to all at the table? First, let's ensure you have a good mindset. When you are having a feast and inviting guests, you prepare both the seats and the table. We need good data and AI to feed the systems, and we need good things feeding our IQ and EQ. We will return to mindset in the book's concluding chapter in more detail, but it is important to note here that having the mindset that you have a place at the table and that you can develop is key.

Now, we need to create an inviting and welcome space for those who want to have a seat at the table. Have you ever had an experience in your career or life where you felt you were being shut out? Maybe you didn't feel you had the background for it, or someone made a comment that turned you away from wanting to even try? Maybe you were the one who turned someone away. As data and AI advance, we need to ensure all feel the welcoming invitation to participate. For those who are leaders, this is an even bigger initiative for you.

Another thing to remember is that data and AI need to be available to all, irrespective of background, race, and so forth. We need to empower skills across organizations. We need to have cultures that help us thrive in our career. We need to have our own seat at the table, and we can empower others to sit down. We can't have the table feeling exclusive and benefiting one group more than another. We also can exclude ourselves in our careers from the table. But, we want to allow all to participate, and therefore need to be accountable for making this happen.

So, how can we help create that seat at the table for all? There are some ways listed below:

- **Build your knowledge.** One of the things we can do is build out our knowledge base. Read, study, learn. Whether it is podcasts, articles, or books, find the ways you can learn and develop. Having a strong knowledge foundation is key to helping you and others find their place at the table. It is like me trying to teach someone how to become an electrician. Please don't come to me for electrician knowledge, I don't have it. If I want a seat at that table, I need to study it. However, don't wait too long to join the table. Don't wait until you feel like you have deep knowledge to sit there. Join and ask lots of questions.
- **Create a friendly, inviting environment.** If you are already fairly familiar with data and/or AI, this is more of a task for you. Don't sit back and make people feel they aren't welcome. If you have some knowledge, be open to sharing it. This may be uncomfortable as you may be introverted, like I am, but take the time to help others with their learning. If you have knowledge and skills that can be shared, do it. Maybe it just takes a friendly person to help some feel like they have a place at the table.
- **Data and AI governance:** One area that should be considered in relation to our formula is data and AI governance. How are the data and AI being governed at our organization? Do we even know if our organization has a data and AI governance program? If we don't know if it does, find out. If it does, study and learn it. If it doesn't, build one. Data and AI governance covers accessibility, who has access to what, and the fair and ethical use of data. How do we ensure ethical use plus equitable access across the organization? Don't just guess, build this governing framework for success.
- **Create data and AI literacy programs:** Work toward building a good data and AI literacy program in your organization. Everyone has some data literacy skills, which is a good thing, but we need to upskill and/or reskill people to truly have success at the table. If we don't, we may cause inequity to grow. Work to empower people.

A Note of Caution

Now, I want to add a cautionary note. As I mentioned at the beginning of this chapter, overreliance on AI is not necessarily a good thing. Let us return to the analogy of working our critical thinking muscles like going to the gym. When a person works out, they can develop strong and better muscles. When they stop working out for a period of time, the muscles lose strength. Don't let this happen to your cognitive muscles; we need to retain our unique ability to think intelligently and act according to our conscience.

According to the Forbes article "Your Brain on AI: Atrophied and Unprepared," a Carnegie Mellon University and Microsoft study looked at 319 professionals and found that while AI can reduce the mental effort required for a task, it may lead to diminished critical engagement.[9] The article notes: "62 percent of participants reported engaging in less critical thinking when using AI, particularly in routine or lower-stakes tasks." The study also found that those with more confidence in their own knowledge were 27 percent more likely to critically assess the outputs of AI, rather than accept them without question. Evaluating AI outputs is a very important task within AI literacy, which we will dive into in Chapter 4.

To work your cognitive muscles so that AI doesn't undermine your abilities and instead augments your journey to success, you can do the following activities:

- **Do "deep work"**: Deep work is defined as "the capacity for concentrated, high-quality cognitive activities demanding deep focus, creativity, and problem-solving."[10] According to Cal Newport's book *Deep Work*, our brains have capacity for four hours of deep work a day (a study by Anders Ericsson, a psychologist, suggests the same).[11] So, allow yourself time to do deep work during your day. For me, deep work can be journaling in the morning, reading and studying, or even when I write a book. Tire those thinking muscles. Work hard on it.
- **Create moments of reflection**: Meditation can be a powerful way to focus on a subject and to take time to understand things, so ensure you are creating moments in your life to reflect. As you

build your knowledge within data and AI, reflect on what you are studying and think of areas where it can be applied.

- **Shut down distraction:** Are you ever guilty of doomscrolling or sitting on your phone too long? I am! We have the ability to sit on our phones and look at social media, read Reddit, answer emails, read the news. We may have many streaming services at our disposal. We may have busy jobs and hundreds of emails and texts coming through. Let's shut down the distraction we are feeling in our lives so that we can do the "deep work."
- **Read:** I love to read, whether that be physical books or listening to audiobooks. Books on data, AI, critical thinking or emotional intelligence, for example, are very useful tools to strengthen cognitive muscles.
- **Study:** Although books are part of this, learning from podcasts, TED/TEDx talks, learning videos, and online or in-person courses can add variety to your learning and keep your cognitive muscles engaged.
- **Journal:** Journaling is important to me, and I recommend it as a way to record what you are learning. Write how things apply to you in your job. For example, when studying data visualization, figure out the best way to utilize visualizations for data success in your career, or if you are working in a spreadsheet analyzing information, write ways you could analyze it differently. Write down questions you want to ask and then do the research, ask experts in the space, or even use generative AI to answer those questions. Keep digging deeper, writing, and critically evaluating the response the AI gave you. What questions should you ask? Well, it can be "why" or "what." You could ask the "how" to dig in and learn processes more.
- **Block your calendar to implement the above practices:** Block off your calendar for critical thinking. Set aside maybe 30–60 minutes a day to journal, read, reflect, and practice data and AI principles. Create personal opportunities and take accountability to grow these areas in your life.

Organization Success: Data- and AI-Driven Culture

For an organization to thrive with Engineered Intelligence, they must help individuals succeed in their own seat at the table by putting in place a positive culture. Let's look at each of the key pillars of culture, both individually and organizationally, to see how they help Engineered Intelligence to thrive:

- **Pillar 1: Fluency**: For people to thrive at the table with Engineered Intelligence, fluency (the ability to speak the language of data and AI) can empower them. Remember our terms at the beginning and turn to Chapter 9 for more information on communication.
- **Pillar 2: Iteration**: Organizations need to work toward a mindset of iteration and not perfection. We need to be iterating on the work we are doing to keep it moving forward. Don't stress if the analysis isn't perfect, that is okay. We have the culture that allows us to pivot and succeed.
- **Pillar 3: Community**: Whether at your organization or in your career, find ways to create a community that fosters conversation and insights sharing. Then, we are learning from others.
- **Pillar 4: DNA of Data and AI**: Helping everyone understand that they aren't needing to become data scientists or machine learning engineers can help them feel more confident. Instead, weave the DNA of data and AI work throughout the organization.
- **Pillar 5: Learn Fast**: I don't like the phrase "fail fast." Even if they say the organization has a goal or mantra to fail fast, most bosses aren't paying a nice bonus to someone who has failed in a project. Instead, let's adopt the phrase "learn fast." Experiment, iterate, and learn fast.
- **Pillar 6: Data and AI Skepticism**: One thing we should be doing is being a skeptic of data and AI. Healthy skepticism means questioning things. It doesn't mean that things are wrong. Instead, we are just questioning it. One thing this also means is that we need to allow our work to be questioned. How comfortable are you having your work questioned? If you aren't, allow it to happen.

Culture is a good way, whether your own personal culture or the organization's culture, to help Engineered Intelligence to be a thing. Don't allow the old way of doing things to get in the way of the new.

Conclusion

Our formula is: Data + AI + IQ + EQ = Engineered Intelligence. We all have a place at this table, we need to find it, take a seat, and ensure we have the skills to help us succeed. Gaining confidence in using data and AI isn't all about just having the data and AI in front of us. It is about having all four parts of our equation be a part of our decision making. We are engineering intelligence to drive outcomes and objectives. Engineered Intelligence can empower our decision making greatly, so allow it.

KEY TAKEAWAYS

- Remember our formula: Data + AI + IQ + EQ = Engineered Intelligence.
- You have the ability to utilize each of the four components of the formula.
- The four rights of data are: the RIGHT data, at the RIGHT time, for the RIGHT objective, with the RIGHT literacy.
- The three Cs of data literacy are: curiosity, creativity, and critical thinking.
- Remember, data has been around for a long time.
- AI may be surrounded by hype and buzz, but it also has tangible value.
- Don't allow your cognitive muscles to atrophy. Continue to study and use those muscles.

Notes

1 C. Westfall. The Dark Side of AI: Tracking the Decline of Human Cognitive Skills, *Forbes*, December 18, 2024, www.forbes.com/sites/chriswestfall/2024/12/18/the-dark-side-of-ai-tracking-the-decline-of-human-cognitive-skills/ (archived at https://perma.cc/6FSH-2MVJ)

2 T. Well. The Decline of Critical Thinking Skills, *Psychology Today*, July 5, 2023, www.psychologytoday.com/us/blog/the-clarity/202306/the-decline-of-critical-thinking-skills (archived at https://perma.cc/6LFP-KTLY)

3 P. Vadapalli. The History of AI: A Chronology of Key Innovations and Milestones in Artificial Intelligence, upGrad, February 21, 2025, www.upgrad.com/blog/the-history-of-ai/ (archived at https://perma.cc/2PTW-M5BY)

4 M. Michalowski. How Much Data Is Generated Every Day in 2025? Spacelift, July 10, 2025, spacelift.io/blog/how-much-data-is-generated-every-day (archived at https://perma.cc/XH5B-PPWS)

5 S. Shatby. The History of Data: From Ancient Times to Modern Day, 365 DataScience, April 15, 2024, 365datascience.com/trending/history-of-data/ (archived at https://perma.cc/95H4-5QYH)

6 Utah State University. John Graunt (1620 – 1674), www.usu.edu/math/schneit/StatsHistory/EarlyDataAnalysts/Graunt (archived at https://perma.cc/ZF3F-EVCD)

7 *Psychology Today* Staff. Emotional Intelligence, www.psychologytoday.com/us/basics/emotional-intelligence (archived at https://perma.cc/5LEU-PJSV)

8 *Psychology Today* Staff. Dunning-Kruger Effect, www.psychologytoday.com/us/basics/dunning-kruger-effect (archived at https://perma.cc/JM2B-PFTD)

9 L. Daniel. Your Brain on AI: "Atrophied and Unprepared," *Forbes*, February 14, 2025, www.forbes.com/sites/larsdaniel/2025/02/14/your-brain-on-ai-atrophied-and-unprepared-warns-microsoft-study/ (archived at https://perma.cc/YYA4-JXRH)

10 A. Nortje. Deep Work: The Book, the Meaning & the Author, PositivePsychology.com, September 14, 2023, positivepsychology.com/deep-work/ (archived at https://perma.cc/Z8Y7-WW5V)

11 I. Gupta. Can We Really Do Deep Work More than 6 Hours a Day? Understand the Secret Behind It, Pesto, www.pesto.tech/resources/can-we-really-do-deep-work-more-than-6-hours-a-day (archived at https://perma.cc/E2N9-GURQ)

2

What Does Data and AI Confidence Look Like?

To jump into this chapter, let's define confidence. I am going to do it from a personal perspective, and not go to a formal definition. To do so, let's take a look at learning to ride a bike. When you first ride a bike, you may start off with training wheels that help to stabilize and keep the bike upright. At first, even then, you may not have all the confidence in the world riding the bike, but you can go and use it fairly well. Then, you take the training wheels off and someone may hold the bike seat for you. You feel uneasy on the bike like this, but you feel assured because someone is holding the bike. Like with training wheels, you had confidence because something was holding you up.

Finally, the person lets go and the nerves and anxiousness can kick in. You don't want to do it without the confidence, but you need to jump in and own the "no training wheels" bike. Eventually, you can ride on your own. What's funny is, you can go for a time without doing so, but if you jump back on the bike, you may just gain confidence quickly. You learned how to do it and then you were able to go. You then had freedom getting around and being able to do more.

With data and AI, you may have "training wheels" to begin with, and that is okay. You have something there to stabilize you as you learn how to go. Then, you take the training wheels off and have a mentor at your side helping you get value from data and AI. Finally, the mentor may "step aside," even though they may still be around for help and advice, like with riding a bike. You are able to move forward and utilize data and AI with more confidence. You can turn to others for help, but you have gained confidence to utilize data and AI in your life and career. You have been given access to tools that can help you be more effective and efficient.

This definition helps us to put together, albeit over time, the puzzle of data and AI confidence. I mean, if you have a puzzle with thousands of different pieces, you don't just dump the pieces on the table and *poof*, it is magically put together. No, you take time to put it together. Data and AI confidence isn't a puzzle that you dump on the table and magic happens. It takes time, unless you are Harry Potter and can wave a magic wand for insight.

Now, I want you to think for a minute about your background, specifically your education. Did you get a degree in data or AI or a related field? Do you feel confident that your background empowers you to succeed with data and AI? Maybe you do and that is great. We can still help you with your data and AI journey, providing you with tools and strategies to continue your learning. If you don't feel confident, that is okay too, as this book will help you along the way. Remember, you have a seat at the table, no matter what your previous experience is.

Now, let's start building our puzzle.

When you saw my definition of confidence, did anything stick out to you? Let's start with the term "training wheels." Confidence is a feeling you have stability and something to hold you up while you are learning. In data and AI, training wheels may be books or courses teaching you what to do. They may be an AI assistant helping you along the journey. What are your feelings about data and AI training wheels? Can you think of any that can be there for you? A mentor may be a good place to start.

Let's now look at a mentor holding you up as your progress, teaching and talking to you so you can be guided on your data and AI journey. Through building your data and AI skills, you can approach the world of data and AI with a support system at your side, helping you to not "fall off." You have the power to create confidence in your ability to succeed with data and AI, utilizing the power and knowledge of others.

The second part of my definition suggests a belief that one will act in the right or effective way to support you. This is trust and confidence in those around you to help you succeed. Well, I will also say that this means that you should be a sponsor and support for all on the data and AI journey. In the world of data and AI, where things can be misused and biases exist, the ability to work in a community with others can help provide one with confidence. Now, to ensure we will work in the correct and effective way, we can develop the mindset that we will aim to work in collaboration with others. Although you will inevitably make mistakes throughout the journey, being well-intentioned will build your confidence and set you up for success. Having people in place to help you succeed, to help you understand where things may have gone wrong in an analysis or prompt, can help you find your success.

A third part of my definition is when you are left to work on your own. This may be the most intimidating part when riding a bike, except for the first time you step up on it. When left on your own, you are trusted that you can safely go it alone. Trust is a key word within data and AI. Why would we work with data and AI if we do not have trust in them, or in those who use them? Trust in the data and AI means that the data is accurate, the AI isn't making things up (hallucinating), and that we have confidence in using both to make and implement decisions in our careers. Trust that we can do what we need to do, and our colleagues can do what they need to do. In our case of data and AI confidence, we need to trust in our own ability to use data and AI.

One thing to hit on with AI was mentioned in the previous paragraph: hallucination. AI can hallucinate, meaning it makes up its outputs. We can look at the prompt response and think it is right, but in reality it was entirely made up. When riding a bike, do parents sometimes tell the kid they are going to hold onto the bike and then just let go, without the kid knowing it? What happens when the kid realizes the parent isn't there? The confidence is shaken. AI makes things up, and then we can lose confidence in it. But, if we take the time to understand that AI can potentially hallucinate, we can recognize that it is happening and we don't have to use the output, we don't have to fear having someone let go. We can utilize our critical thinking muscles each time we receive a prompt response. Then, when we find it was hallucinating, we prompt again, possibly push back against the AI and its response, and then keep working forward.

There are two important points worth mentioning. Returning to our Chapter 1 discussion, you should continually ensure your cognitive muscles are working and growing so you continue to trust your ability and therefore continue on your journey with data and AI confidence. Do not forget to critically think about the data and AI. The reality is, if we become complacent, we may lose confidence in our abilities as the world of data and AI moves rapidly.

Secondly, don't be hard on yourself. If you don't know how to use data or AI well, that's okay. I have five kids. They didn't all start walking on day one. When they started walking, they stumbled. Learning a new skill is a process. Eventually, they walked and now some drive. Remember that new skills take time to develop and are a process.

One thing I have said in the past when coaching in sports is that I don't like the phrase "practice makes perfect," because you can practice something incorrectly and develop habits that aren't so perfect. Then it may be hard to unbreak those habits. Instead, let's use the phrase "practice makes permanent." Let's work on our confidence and skills, let's build trust in ourselves to have our seat at the table and adopt the right mindset to develop and grow in data and AI. I don't want you to feel burdened or in any way lesser because you aren't where others are on this journey.

Crucially, we need to establish why you should want confidence and skills in data and AI.

The reality is that the AI train is moving, and it is not slow. It is hurtling down the track at an incredible pace. Also, there is more data today than maybe ever on the planet. Overall, data and AI are here, and the future is unknown. However, when we develop confidence and skills to use data and AI, that can empower us to be a part of the future and not a bystander watching it go by. That is a big thing to think about.

As I have been writing this book, there has been much written or said about the negative impacts of AI in the future. Are jobs going to be eliminated? What about knowledge workers, will they have a place? They aren't building machines, but instead they are working on strategy, accounting, marketing; things that are typically done by a human. AI could threaten this. Also, are students just cheating their way through the education system?

With this negative hype and news around us, developing data and AI confidence can empower you to see beyond the negativity and utilize data and AI more effectively. You may be able to make smarter decisions in the workplace, leading to bonuses or even promotions, or you may be able to get rid of some of the mundane work you do, so your role becomes more enjoyable. You may become more creative with AI as your partner. Overall, data and AI are important to not only to business, but to us. Let's ensure we are a part of the data and AI journey and not fading into the background.

Principles of Learning

One thing to focus on as you build your confidence is how to continue on your learning path. In this section of the book, I am going to share the principles of learning and tie them to the four pillars of our formula: data, AI, human intelligence, and emotional intelligence. We will look at how you can attack these pillars with learning principles. Now, don't feel like you have to do each of these principles. Find the ones that work for you and go with them. Make your journey with this book, with data and AI enjoyable. If you don't enjoy it, you may not gain the confidence you desire.

For my principles of learning, we will explore some from different sources. Let's start with principles from the American Psychological Association[1] that I have adjusted for you.

Personal Perception Matters

This means that how we view intelligence, learning, and our own ability can help to shape us and affect learning. How do you feel about yourself and your ability to learn? Do you feel strong and confident, or do you find yourself talking negatively about your abilities and intelligence, like you just can't "do" data and AI? Perception matters.

One thing I have done for a long time is walk my elementary children to school, when I can. With my youngest two I will ask something like: "what can you do?" And they respond: "amazing things." Do you think that about yourself? When you are learning, ensure you have a belief in yourself and your capabilities. Without it, it will make it very hard to have data and AI confidence.

What We Already Know Affects Our Learning

When we have existing knowledge, this can impact our view of new information or existing information because our personal bias can get in the way of how we view it. So, how do we make sure our current knowledge is conducive to learning new information?

One key aspect of this is to have good emotional intelligence and self-awareness: you may not know everything or that the information you do already know may shift and change, and that's okay. We need to be open to the idea that we could be wrong. One thing to do is leave emotions at the door: don't allow emotions to dictate the facts. Allow the data and facts to influence your decisions instead. Also, make sure you are critically thinking and reflecting on your knowledge. If we set our minds in the past, we may set ourselves up to fail.

Learning Is Based on Context

Bringing context to learning matters, so that we don't just retain information but know how to use it. Within data and AI, context can matter greatly. In fact, it may be one of the most important things we include with data and AI. We should be asking ourselves: "what is a problem I am trying to solve?" or "what does this data show us and how does it impact the question/s we are working on?" Then, research if there is a data and AI solution for it. Within my career, I can share an example of how having context in the data I was sharing at my organization mattered.

I was working for a financial institution during the financial crisis in 2007–08 that hit America and affected other parts of the world. I had to deliver a PowerPoint report to people in the organization that looked at delinquency rates and write-offs. The problem was that it was a large PowerPoint presentation, I think over 70 slides long. It was a stressful report, given the Chief Risk Officer of the company received it. The slides included many charts. I broke the charts down into six total charts that could be viewed on a mobile phone.

I was eventually given the go ahead from my SVP to just deliver the six charts. Guess how many requests I received for the longer report? I don't remember a single one. Instead, because my six charts had the context in them and the info needed was there, things were good. Remember, context matters, so ensure your data and AI work has it.

Acquiring Long-Term Knowledge and Skills Is a Long Game, Not a Short Game

Run the marathon, don't just sprint. If we sit and read about a topic and think we have solved the problem at that moment in time, we can be happy about it, but the race isn't finished. Instead, you go onto another topic, and another, like you complete one mile, then the next. It is the continuous forward movement that is going to matter. Practice makes permanent. To continue our analogy of the marathon, although the training can be long, difficult, and painful, the feeling of satisfaction when finishing is great. The same is true in the long game of learning data and AI for confidence.

To keep moving forward effectively in your data and AI journey, ensure you are pacing yourself consistently. Having a routine can help with consistency. Routine is a good thing to develop, as it sets you up for accomplishment, and we will discuss this later in this chapter.

Intrinsic vs. Extrinsic Motivation

We may think that outside incentives push us to learn or do more. AI and data could garner external rewards, such as praise, a bigger salary, or a better bonus. Yet, while external rewards are wonderful, they aren't everything. While rewards for studying and learning may be nice, they aren't the thing that is going to help us the most. Intrinsically wanting to do something and working toward something matters more, as motivation can ebb.

Ensure you are picking topics within data and AI that you are intrinsically motivated to study. When you have picked these, then you can march forward with your intrinsic reason for studying them, as well as your motivation that is most likely driven by an external reward.

Personally, I enjoy chatting about AI. I enjoy reading about it. I enjoy writing books. There is an intrinsic reason there. You probably have things you are excited about and talk about. That's great. Find areas in data and AI you can be excited about. It will be easier to develop your data and AI confidence this way.

Let's turn to a few more principles from the Knowledge Academy.[2] One thing to note is that some of these principles may not resonate with you, which is fine. Your job is to figure out how you learn so you can develop skills in data and AI to increase your confidence. To note, I have modified these for this book's reader, because these principles were originally intended for students and teachers.

Network and Interact

Network and interact with others to help you learn. Find people who know the subjects in data and AI you want to learn from and don't be shy. Ask questions, connect with them in person at networking events, or online, for example on LinkedIn.

Your network is a key tool. I have found success through my network. Throughout my career in data literacy, I had people who bought into my work. Data literacy was something I was helping to build. From the person hiring me, to being invited to events around the world, to someone telling me I need to be active on LinkedIn, I was given a support system that helped me thrive. This wasn't just me doing it, but multiple people helping me and bringing the work to life. Ensure you are building your network and utilizing it for learning and development.

As I write this book, I have been able to deliver multiple events, and for one in particular, the feedback was good and that helped me to develop confidence in what I am doing. Who doesn't like receiving positive feedback? We like to receive it, but we should also be active voices that speak up about people in our networks.

Set High Expectations and Think Big

Dream big. Set high learning expectations for yourself, but make them so they are achievable. You do not want to set unrealistic goals that will have a negative effect on your confidence.

One thing you gain by having high expectations is the progress you make along the way. With high expectations, you may not hit the highest point, but what about the skills you develop on the way to the top? Achieving most on the way versus completing a small expectation is much more effective. Like losing weight or building muscle, you may not see the gains immediately, but if you look at the picture over time, you may have a nicely built picture.

One thing you can do to set your high expectations is to write down what having your desired level of expertise in data and AI would look like. What skills would you have? What would you be able to do? How often would you be studying? What would your routine look like?

Allow for Feedback

Feedback is a good mechanism that can empower us to learn and grow. We could be learning the wrong things if we don't seek feedback in our learning. Now, you may ask: how can I receive feedback if I am learning and studying, especially if I am doing this journey on my own?

One way you can receive feedback is to find yourself a mentor or accountability partner, someone whom you can trust to give you honest feedback. Make sure you aren't just fed with positivity. At the gym, you put your muscles under stress with weights so they can grow. The same can happen with feedback. Now, that doesn't mean you need to be belittled or torn down. Instead, find someone who will give you the feedback constructively, so you can build your data and AI skills.

Another way to get feedback is to take courses and assessments. Invest in yourself and find opportunities to test what level your skills are at and, more importantly, where your gaps are. The gaps are an area of learning opportunity. In fact, an assessment could be a good way for you to start your data and AI learning journey. If you don't know where to find a course or assessment, use a search engine like Google or even search in a generative AI model. Following the assessment, you can build your roadmap to where you want to go.

Now, let's look at three more principles, devised by me.

The Three Cs of Data Literacy—Curiosity, Creativity, Critical Thinking

These are my three Cs, and we should utilize them not just with data and AI, but in our lives.

In the realm of learning, the ability to be curious and ask questions is key. Questions can spark development, new pathways to learning, and help one succeed with data and AI. You don't necessarily need to be able to do all the work after you have the answer, either. It may be left to a data professional to do something about it, but make sure you are asking a lot of questions.

The second C is creativity. Allow your creativity to thrive. Sometimes data and AI topics may be boring. That's okay. To overcome this, you can be creative in your question asking and how you study, for example.

The third C is critical thinking. The ability to critically assess a topic openly and deeply, ask more questions, and learn more is key. This human cognitive skill is important to keep whilst working with data and AI. So, as you are learning, ask if things could be done differently. Don't just accept things as they are because you may discover a better solution. Just like I shifted the larger PowerPoint presentation to six slides, you can think through new solutions that may make your life easier. It may have been that that example was one of curiosity, creativity, and critical thinking.

Build a Routine

Have you ever set out to do something, but you didn't have a routine or a set way you were doing it, which made it a lot harder? Did you get frustrated and struggle with your goal? Now, let's flip this and ask: have you ever achieved something whilst having a routine, and what was the outcome?

In the sports world, you can look at the consistency of holding regular practices. Think about fitness and how consistency plays a role in what you achieve. If you have goals to hit a certain weight on the bench press or to lose a certain amount of weight, and you are consistent within a routine, you are more set up for success.

For me, people have been astonished by what I am able to get done. It isn't a secret. My routine helps. I am a morning person, up early. My routine helps me thrive. If you are looking to have gains and build confidence and skills in data and AI, have a routine of daily learning or growth. Mark it down and succeed.

Build a Roadmap

Build yourself a good roadmap. Back before our phones could be our maps, you may have had to plan ahead for how you would get to your destination, or have a physical map handy with you. You could tick things off on the map as you traveled along. Then, you reached your destination. For our roadmaps of personal confidence and skill building, what milestones can you tick off along the way? Maybe you hit a milestone and celebrate with a trip to your favorite coffee shop or day at the spa. Maybe you find as you journey that your milestones aren't big enough, and so you take on bigger goals and tasks. Build a roadmap and celebrate your success.

The book *Legacy* by James Kerr says that the better your structure, the better your strategy.[3] The weaker your structure the weaker your strategy. This is important to remember as we go along our data and AI journey: we want to achieve a certain level of skill and confidence but if we aren't structured in our manner of getting there, how can we hope to achieve what we want effectively?

If you are new to the field, studying machine learning engineering might not be the place to start. Instead, starting with the basics of machine learning will be much more useful. Then, set milestones for yourself to work toward your goal.

Your Framework: Routine

In this section of the chapter, I am going to provide a framework for building an effective routine for learning. By establishing a routine and being consistent, you will start to gain more confidence in data and AI.

For me, routine is key to my success in getting things done, and I have outlined this below:

- **Wake up early:** Now, I understand that not everyone is a morning person, and I get that. With that in mind, don't focus on waking up early as much as being consistent with your time set out to accomplish tasks. If you are a night person, maybe set aside 30 minutes before bed for your routine. Find what works for you. For me, the early wake up time is when I take care of things. At the end of a long or busy day, I don't find it as easy to complete tasks as I do in the mornings with a clearer mind. (Plus, with five kids, getting things done before everyone wakes up is helpful for me!) My ability to get work done in the morning and thrive helps me to read and study, to journal, and write my books.
- **Consistent location:** Every morning, I know where I am going to sit down and read and journal. My puppy will come and sit next to me as I do so. My brain is conditioned to know that if I wake up and sit in that spot, I will be journaling and reading. That is great. That consistent spot is where I go for my routine. For you, find a consistent spot where you can study, learn, meditate, whatever it may be. Condition your brain for success. Find a place where you know you can go, and consistently use it.
- **Sound:** This doesn't necessarily need to be music; it could be white noise or silence. I turn calmer music on that I find on YouTube. This is nice to have on in the background.
- **My puppy:** My dog lies next to me on the couch as I read and journal. You may not have a pet, but anything that you enjoy, such as your favorite hot drink, is useful. If I have my dog with me, I enjoy myself more. Having that positive influence can be something that helps me to be happier—and being happier means we will be more likely to do something.
- **Put your phone away:** This is one I need to do more than I do currently. If your phone is next to you, you may be tempted to pick it up and scroll—and why wouldn't we? The dopamine hits can

help us feel good. However, if it is distracting us from our end goal, it is something to put aside, especially as it can be a big time drain.

- **Consistency:** We have used this word numerous times throughout this chapter, but it really is key. Implement this routine every day—even if you don't adhere to it perfectly, being consistently good is better overall than just having moments of greatness.

These are components of my own morning routine, but for you it may be different. So, how do you find what works for you? Experimentation! You may think you're not a morning person and you try it out for a bit, and you find that you like it. Or you find a set hour of time in the evening.

What matters is that you find out what works for you, and you implement that in your life. Then, be consistent with it and build your data and AI confidence.

Your Framework: Building Your Roadmap

I have written a roadmap below that can be used to help you achieve your goals so that you can become more confident with data and AI.

To help us with our roadmap building, I have adapted the "11 Steps to Building a Learning and Development Strategy" from training and development specialists the Colin James Method:[4]

Step 1: Alignment

Align your personal goal for learning data and AI. To figure out what your goal should be, you can start by asking yourself questions such as "What do I want to learn?", "Which topics in data and AI interest me?", "Do I know anyone who can help me on this journey?", and "What gaps do I currently have in my skill-set?" It could be the skill you want to learn is to have greater prompt ability with AI. Set that as your goal and get to work.

For example, if you aspire to become a senior leader in your organization, you need to consider the current trends of AI and understand their potential business applications. This is because they may need to be implemented by the time you step into a senior role in order for the business to maintain a competitive advantage. Having a forward-thinking approach with AI means that you will have more confidence to pitch the use of these tools in your organization. Furthermore, learning about data and AI isn't always about the specifics of these technologies. You could also aim to develop your ability to lead others using data and AI in their careers, or how to become more adaptable and innovative, using data and AI to solve business problems.

Now, remember, you are thinking big but that doesn't mean your goals should be placed out of reach. Instead, you can create multiple roadmaps along the way. Think of our senior leader example above—before achieving this goal, it is likely that you will need to achieve one or two promotions to reach that role.

Step 2: Determine Your Personal Skills

Assessing ourselves is a good thing to do as you build your roadmap and start your journey. When you have selected your goal for this roadmap you then need to know what you should be studying and learning. If you just pick up a book on data and AI, you may read it and find you already know some of the information, or you may find it to be too advanced for you. Overall, a skills gap analysis is a good way to determine gaps and where to go.

Now, you may ask yourself: how can I build this assessment? You can use generative AI to do so; have it build an assessment and score the assessment. Tell it to build roadmaps for the skills you are lacking. Have it prioritize them. Remember to not only focus on your areas of need, but focus also on your strengths and ask AI how to improve those even more.

Step 3: Create a Learning Journey with Milestones

Your roadmap should be structured, with a timeline denoting milestones along the way, and the finish point. If you don't have a timeline, you may find you can become complacent around your learning and you will never achieve your goal. During your set timeframe, break things down even further. For example, you could set yourself a target of one chapter every three days, or one learning video every week.

Along with that, you can give yourself rewards as you achieve the milestones. Maybe it is grabbing a certain treat you like or buying something that you have wanted for a while. Remember that this journey should be enjoyable.

Step 4: Set Your Routine

Now that you have a journey in front of you, what routine is going to get you there? Follow the routine framework in the previous section to help with this, because, as I stated above, being consistent will help you achieve your goal more effectively than just doing your learning from time to time. You could create time blocks on your daily calendar for working toward your goal. That's okay. Sometimes we need to say no to other things and prioritize ourselves. Eliud Kipchoge may be the world's greatest ever marathon runner, and he didn't rely on a diet or miracle to succeed. He says we need "vitamin N."[5] Vitamin N is the ability to say no. Saying no to things is easier said than done, but we can be more disciplined in what we take on. If something is not helping us achieve our goals, we are hindering our forward progress.

Step 5: Utilize Different Learning Mediums

Don't like podcasts? That's alright, read a book. Don't like to read? That's okay, watch a TED Talk. There are so many different learning mediums to use on your journey, and utilizing these will help you succeed by keeping your mind engaged and ensuring an enjoyable learning journey.

Step 6: Get Started

This may seem silly, but it is a crucial step. When you have your roadmap complete and you are ready to go, start your journey and execute. Use that vitamin N and move forward. Say no to things that stand in the way. It could be a work project that seems great, but isn't tied to the priorities you want to work on. A simple example is saying no to the treat that hinders you toward your personal health goals. Adopt that mindset to work and your career. Also, you are going to get advice in your career, and guess what—it won't all be good advice. Take the time to listen and understand it, but then think about whether it fits or not. If the advice fits, great, and if it doesn't, then move past it.

Step 7: Take Notes and/or Journal

One thing I encourage you to do is to journal and/or take notes on your data and AI confidence learning journey. Write how things you are learning could be applied in your career and then test it out. Take notes on new skills you want to learn or have discovered.

Now, notes don't have to be handwritten all the time. Instead, you can also have voice notes and use those. It could be that you are on a walk and an idea comes to you. Instead of stopping and pulling out paper and a pen, which you may not carry anyway, record a voice note. Then, in your routine, take some time to review the voice notes. If you want to, write them down.

Step 8: Feedback Loop, Iteration, and the Next Journey

The final step is your feedback loop, iteration, and the next journey. A feedback loop is a mechanism you can use to gather feedback and then iterate and move forward. It is a space to allow feedback, and it is your job to not ignore the feedback. It may not all apply, so ensure you critically think about the feedback, but take it and iterate. Like working out in the gym, if you feel a new pain that something is off, you shouldn't just ignore it. Instead, listen to that message and adjust. Similarly, we need to allow feedback to come to us and we can make adjustments.

Think back to the learning principle "Allow for feedback." A feedback loop is a way for you to receive feedback and therefore monitor your progress effectively. You could utilize AI, a friend, a partner, or a mentor to be your feedback loop. Remember to be open to negative feedback. If all the feedback we receive is positive, how is that going to help us? We need to know where we can improve so we can become more knowledgeable, more confident, and help us find where we can grow.

You may need to reestablish your goal and iterate upon it. That is okay. Don't let change knock your data and AI confidence. Instead, look at the change and evolution as positive. You may be changing your mindset and therefore diving in more powerfully and succeeding. You may be pivoting your career goal. You may be evolving so that AI is just becoming a part of your everyday life, like a smartphone or the internet. Can you imagine your life without the internet? Now, can you build your confidence in data and AI so you can't imagine your life without them?

With this new information from the feedback loop, the next thing you can do is go on another journey. What do you want to learn next? You can then keep your learning as a continual journey of development and not a finish line.

> If you go down the mentor route, find those whose values, ideas, and mentorship align with you and can challenge you. Don't find mentors that are just there to say "yes." If all they do is agree with you, you may not grow. They may be saying things you want to hear and not saying things you *need* to hear. Find those who will challenge your thoughts and ideas, who can get the best out of you, and who can help you create the career you want and not just a job title.

Conclusion

Ask yourself this question: what does data and AI confidence look like to you? Remember our analogy of learning to ride a bike. It is a journey, and a child rarely just hops on the bike and has no issues. They may struggle, they may start with training wheels and then a support system to hold them up. Even when the support system lets go, confidence can waver. Then, over time, they can develop the confidence to hop on that bike, which can take them places.

Data and AI confidence can be similar. You may have training wheels, support systems, but over time, hopefully, you develop the skills and confidence to allow data and AI to take you to new places. Maybe they take you to places you didn't know you could reach.

KEY TAKEAWAYS

- Data and AI confidence is like learning to ride a bike. We don't learn to ride a bike overnight, and we may not be able to take in all the knowledge and then build all the skills to have full confidence in data and AI overnight. That is okay. Instead, like learning to ride a bike, take the necessary steps to build your confidence in using data and AI.
- Following the steps of building a learning plan can build confidence when studying data and AI topics.
- Curating a routine is very important so that you can develop and progress your data and AI skills.
- There is no one-size-fits-all approach to building a routine, and that's okay. You can develop confidence in data and AI by finding what works for you. Following the framework for your own learning roadmap can set you on the right course.

Notes

1 American Psychological Association. Top 20 Principles for Teaching and Learning, www.apa.org/ed/schools/teaching-learning/top-twenty/ (archived at https://perma.cc/YZ3S-55R2)

2 The Knowledge Academy. 12 Principles of Teaching: The Fundamentals of Successful, The Knowledge Academy, July 8, 2025, www.theknowledgeacademy.com/blog/principles-of-teaching/ (archived at https://perma.cc/76WN-CG3D)

3 J. Kerr (2013) *Legacy: What the All Blacks Can Teach Us About the Business of Life*, Constable & Robinson

4 E. Bagshaw. 11 Steps to Building a Learning & Development Strategy, The Colin James Method, August 5, 2025, colinjamesmethod.com/building-a-learning-and-development-strategy/ (archived at https://perma.cc/G7Q7-8N3P)

5 A. Migue. What is Vitamin N and How Can It Change Our Routine Forever, Brujula Bike, July 2, 2024, en.brujulabike.com/what-is-vitamin-n/ (archived at https://perma.cc/5Y2B-3AH9)

3

Data Literacy: Your Journey Toward Success

I have the nickname "The Godfather of Data Literacy" because I helped to pioneer, invent, and build this entire field. The first book I wrote was titled *Be Data Literate: The Data Literacy Skills Everyone Needs to Succeed*, and that book is now in its second edition. In this chapter, my goal is to help build out the definition of data literacy, discuss the journey it has been on, and help you with a framework to build out your own data literacy going forward.

To help you begin your journey, it is key to understand that not everyone needs to be a data scientist, but everyone can develop confidence and comfort in using data. Data is a powerful thing and something that is an asset for you to use in your career. Think of data as information that is there to help you, just like the internet, a smartphone, or a computer. Those are tools to help you out. Now, you can use data to help you on your journey.

Defining Data Literacy

Where did I get the idea for data literacy? Earlier in my career I worked for American Express, and I owned the training of the end users on what we were building. Now, we were training them on how to use the dashboards, but it didn't include training them on how to use data. So, I built out training on topics like basic statistics. This plan was denied, saying the end users were not ready and maybe this training could take place in the future. But the idea of teaching people to use data did not leave my mind. Then, I was hired at Qlik and given the freedom to be an entrepreneur. I went there, traveled the globe, and helped to build out the world of data literacy.

The definition of data literacy that I utilized while I was at Qlik and have used since is the ability to read, work with, analyze, and communicate with data. I sometimes ask people which of these four characteristics is the most important. What would you say? The majority answer is "communicate," and I have to say no, that's not right. The ability to read data is the most important. The reason is: if you can't read it right, how are you able to do the other three?

Now, what exactly does this definition mean? Well, let's use some real-world examples that will illustrate that you personally are more data literate than you may think.

Example 1

Have you ever gone on a vacation? Or tried to plan a weekend away? Whilst packing, you wanted to know what clothes to wear or bring, so you looked at the weather app on your phone, which provides data points and predictions. You then used those data points and predictions to determine what clothing to pack for your trip.

Once, I demonstrated a poor execution of data literacy. I was traveling to Finland in late November and decided to not pack a heavier coat for the cold. Therefore, using the weather app to make decisions for clothing or plans is an example of data literacy you may not have considered.

Example 2

Have you ever baked something? I have made who knows how many cookies in my lifetime. To make cookies, you utilize and follow data points (the recipe) to help you make the tastiest cookies successfully. Once, one of my sons used salt instead of sugar—this was not the right ingredient listed in the recipe, so the data literacy decision didn't achieve the desired outcome. Again, this is an example of using data to make a decision.

Example 3

Have you ever been in a job or meeting when someone asks a question and you have the data point they need? Or are you the one who asks the question, and you need the data point to help you out?

The Four Characteristics of Data Literacy

The above were three easy examples of data literacy in our lives. Everyone is data literate to some extent, and that's great. Now, how can we advance our data literacy so we are more effective at executing decisions in our careers? We need to know the four key characteristics of data literacy and then apply them. These four characteristics (reading data, working with data, analyzing data and communicating with data) are discussed in turn below.

Reading Data

The ability to read data is the most important characteristic of data literacy. As mentioned, although people often think it is "communicate with data," without being able to read data correctly, how can we work with, analyze it, or communicate it correctly?

The weather app is a prime example of reading data. The data is built for us to use, and we look at the data, understand what it is saying, and interpret the data point in relation to the decision that needs to be made.

In any career, using data matters greatly. There are many ways we use it:

- **In Finance:** When making financial decisions in your personal life, like choosing what to invest in or when buying a house. It can also empower end users to analyze the data through financial statements and find areas or gaps.
- **In Marketing:** You might want to create a new campaign for a new product your organization is launching. You could use demographic

data to understand the target market and therefore find out how best to build the campaign to appeal to them.

- **In Sales:** You could use data for a specific client to understand them, so that you could offer them a solution that could work best for them.
- **In Personal Development:** You can use data on types of learnings that people are using to advance their skills and then apply those skills to yourself. It may be that you don't know what to do, and so you decide you are going to analyze and figure out what others are doing. This enables you to take data and make decisions to empower your decision making on your personal development.

Whatever your field, look for spaces and ideas around where data could help. Remember that data is only a part of the equation, so don't allow it to dictate all of the decision process but allow it to help you be more confident in your decision. Hopefully, you can see you are more data literate than you realized and so you can gain confidence in how you approach data going forward.

Now, does this mean because you have some skills in reading data already that you are comfortable and set? No. It also doesn't mean you need to go so advanced that you become great at statistics or an expert in the more advanced ways to read data. If you want to be more expert in this sense, then do it! But what you should be targeting is advancing your skills so that you become more proficient in using data to execute decision making that you either make or aim to be making on a day-to-day basis. The data literacy framework discussed later in this chapter will be a guide to help you do this.

Working with Data

The second characteristic of being data literate is working with data. How do you approach working with data when your background may not be in a data discipline? Let's explore this.

In the world of data there are many roles: data engineer, data scientist, data analyst, data management, data visualization, chief data officer, and the largest pool of workers: data consumers. To develop your confidence with data and AI, unless you are looking to grow into more technical spaces, know that working with data will not be as in-depth and/or taxing as some of these other roles.

Instead, you will use your skills to analyze and utilize data to make smart decisions. There is something I call the data and AI driven train, shown in Figure 3.1.

Figure 3.1 shows a flow of data to reach the decision and outcomes. On the left-hand side, you have the data itself. You will have those who work with the data to help create it, manage it, and govern it so it can be used. This area is going to be filled with data professionals.

As you follow the arrow, you can see it then leads to the next phase of the train, the analytics phase. (We will look at analytics in more detail when we get to the third characteristic of data literacy.) This is where working with the data will be of particular use to you, from being able to read it and understand it, to being able to find insight and information. Plus, when coupled with artificial intelligence, you can gain even more insight from the data.

From here, you are then looking to help drive decisions and outcomes in your career: how you can utilize your ability to work with data to help you derive better insight and information, then execute better decisions. How many of us wouldn't want to be better with our decision making? Now, this doesn't mean you just allow the data and analytics

FIGURE 3.1 The data and AI driven train

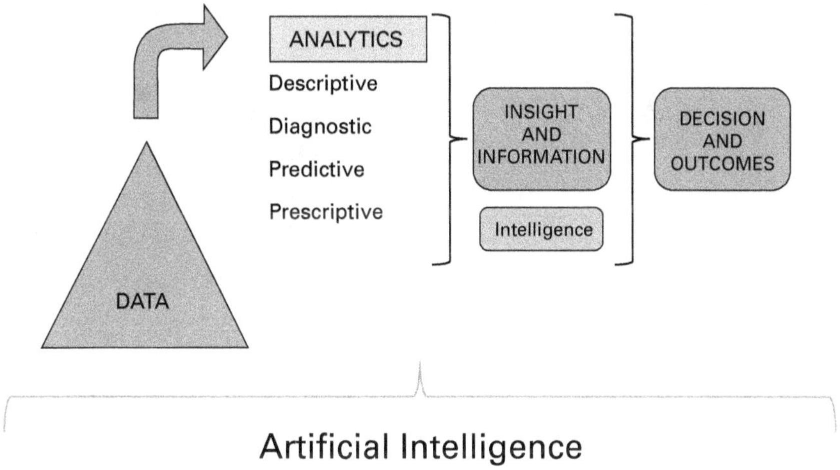

to do all the work. No, you must also bring your human experience and ideas to the table so that you are combining the human and data elements. Our human experience can bring emotion, sympathy, and compassion to what may be a very difficult decision from the data.

For example, say the data says to let go of a certain percentage of the company. The organization would need to be sensitive to the people at risk of redundancy, as well as the other employees affected by the change. Also, what about morale in the culture or the perception of the business externally? These things will need to be managed. Data alone does not account for effects on humans. Therefore, we need to ensure that our personal data points, experience, and emotional intelligence are combined with the data to make decisions.

In our case, to develop more data and AI confidence, learning how you can work with data more effectively is key. Again, deploying the data literacy framework explored later in this chapter will improve your data literacy.

Analyzing Data

As mentioned above, the third characteristic of data literacy is to analyze data. What does it mean to analyze data? It is a process of finding information, insight, and uses in the data. Figure 3.2 outlines the four levels of analytics in my data and AI driven train.

FIGURE 3.2 Four levels of analytics

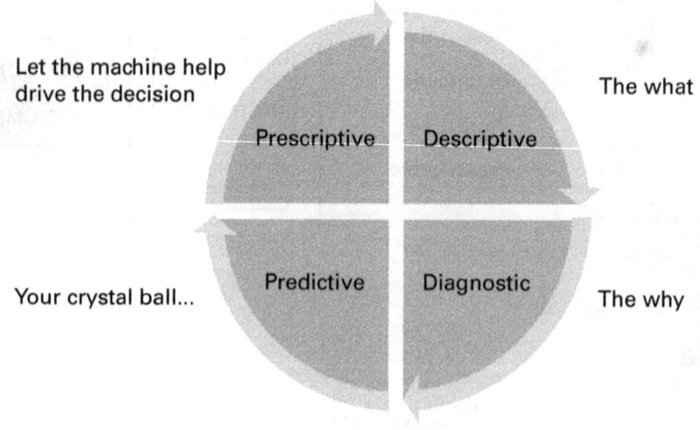

Let's look at each of these four levels with an example. Imagine you are feeling sick. You go to the doctor, and the doctor says to you, you are sick (descriptive), leaves the room and never returns. This is not an effective doctor. If the doctor says: you're sick, and here is why (diagnostic), you have a slightly better doctor. Sometimes, the doctor says: here is why you are sick, and if you follow my advice, such as getting rest and drink lots of water, you should get better (predictive). Finally, the doctor may prescribe something to also help you get better. That is an external influence that helps drive the outcome.

So, where do you fit in with this model? The majority of people will need to hone skills in being able to read data, work with it, and analyze it to find out the "what" and make theories about the "why." Do doctors always get things right? No, they don't. Data analysis won't always get it right, either. You can see the circle of arrows on Figure 3.2. You test out your ideas, generate new ones, and, hopefully, continue to improve over time. From there, you are gleaning information to help you make better decisions.

What about the other two areas: predictive and prescriptive? This is where more advanced and technical skills may be needed. Here, you may have your data scientists or machine learning engineers to help you drive this forward. Plus, with the advancement of AI, it may be that AI will build datasets more and more, and, instead, we interpret them and help make better decisions.

For us all to improve our data literacy skills, let's look at my three Is of the data and AI driven train: information, insight, and intelligence.

Each of these can be important in how we make decisions with data and AI. Information (data) allows us to understand the "what." For example, what is happening with the economy? Insight (derived from this data) is understanding the "why." Why is the economy going this way or that? Finally, intelligence comes from AI. The intelligence may be insight, information, but essentially it is intelligence around something and you can derive it from AI. This means the AI is deriving information or insight for the user that maybe the human didn't see or process; the AI is helping us as a smart intelligent "human."

Communicating with Data

If reading data is the most important characteristic of data literacy, then communicating with data is the secret sauce to data work. Why would I say this? Have you ever had to take your car into a mechanic to have something fixed, but you don't understand the ins and outs of a car so what they say goes over your head? In the world of data and AI, the technical jargon involved may confuse people, so being able to communicate well is important.

It is also important to be able to communicate the value the data and AI are providing to the end user. If we aren't communicating that value accurately and in a way that the person understands, then our insights may fall flat and not be effective. We will discuss communication more in Chapter 9.

This raises a key point about communicating effectively: is all communication verbal? No. In fact, from one study we find that communication is 55 percent nonverbal, 38 percent vocal, and just 7 percent words only.[1] It is therefore important that we work on improving our own body language and our ability to read other people's. If you can read the room and understand that people aren't receiving the message, you know to modify it—whether that be simplifying it or providing definitions.

As much as I like data, the book *How Minds Change* by David McRaney highlights that it isn't data points that will change people's minds; it is narratives.[2] We need to craft messages with data points to support our opinions and ideas; this is called data storytelling. When we don't change our opinions in the face of data, then our data literacy is not working well, and we are being driven by emotions instead of reality.

Although the terms "narrative" or "story" may imply a long or drawn-out message, this isn't the case. We just need to provide sufficient detail so that our specific audience in the organization can make informed decisions.

Data Literacy's Journey

One may ask the question: when will I know I am data literate? This is not an unreasonable question, but is one I hope we eliminate from the conversation. Data literacy itself is a journey that should never end for us. Think about running a race. You spend all this time preparing for the race, putting in the work and effort, and then you run the race, crossing the finish line. You may feel elated and happy. Do you just stop working out altogether after the race? If you did, what would happen? You may lose the gains you created whilst preparing for the race. The same may be said of data literacy. Don't think of there being a finish line, and instead think of data literacy as a life-long quest to empower yourself to succeed in a field that will shift and change. Let's walk you through the journey I have had with data literacy as it has grown and evolved.

The start of my official journey can be traced to late 2015. This is where ideas of what would become data literacy were forming, and in June of 2016, I was hired by Qlik to do a different type of job: create product-agnostic learning frameworks for people about analytics and data principles. At the time, a lot of learning was centered on how to use tools, but not how to use data. This product-agnostic training went well, and little did I know where it would take me and how it would take off. The field of data literacy is still very much applicable (and we also now need to have conversations about AI literacy!).

Data literacy has grown into something big. What we were doing in the beginning is not what we are doing today. There are now tiers for data literacy in an organization. It is a topic that has taken me around the world to speak.

Now, data literacy has both good and bad things about it. When done correctly, data literacy can empower people with new skills, from the ability to read data more effectively to working with it, analyzing it and communicating with it better. When data literacy is done right, organizations can see better decisions being made, which may result in benefits such as higher customer engagement or higher profits. But data literacy has a negative side, too. Critics of data literacy highlight issues like people blaming lack of data literacy on data consumers. The blame game is not something we should be doing. Instead, we should work in a collaborative manner to help facilitate success. Remember, everyone has a seat at the table.

The journey of data literacy has been one that has grown, pivoted, shifted, changed. This requires us as learners and data literacy practitioners to also grow, pivot, shift, and change. When we learn one topic, don't think that topic is done. The areas of data literacy can change, so we need to keep up to date. One example of this change was the advent of generative AI being so usable and consumable. This advancement makes it possible to analyze or use data more easily, but we still need to be vigilant in our evaluation of the responses and whether they are valid. As we progress in our data and AI confidence, have the mindset that this may shift for us and sometimes, yes, we may actually lose skills and abilities in things we have developed. I played volleyball years ago. Could I still play like I did then? No. My skills wouldn't be the same because I switched to rugby.

You may be marching forward enjoying one thing, but don't let that hinder your ability to discover and utilize curiosity to learn different areas. When I was working in the data space, I didn't know I would evolve to help pioneer and invent the space of data literacy. Be open to the shifts and changes that can occur.

A way to ensure your data literacy journey is one that empowers you to succeed is to remain curious, one of the three Cs of data literacy, which are detailed in the next section of this chapter. As you are going through your data literacy journey, allow yourself to be curious about other aspects of learning and growth. You may find that there are areas in data and AI that really interest you, but you may have missed them had you not been curious about them.

In my career, I've been a curious person. Early in my career, I would get interested in other jobs and areas of the business for various reasons. I had at least one leader in the space I worked in who told me I should just focus on one thing. Here's the thing: my career would not have had the same trajectory if I had stayed put.

That said, do you need to be super curious and study everything, all at once? No, aim for progression over a longer period of time. If you try to do everything, you may burn out. (That was a part of my data literacy journey that you should avoid.) If you are early in your career, be curious and go for other roles and skills. Don't just let things sit and stagnate. Be curious, learn, develop, find what suits you.

Having a framework can help you develop and grow moving forward on your journey. Let's jump into this now.

Data Literacy Frameworks

In this section, I am going to give you two frameworks to help you with your data literacy journey. One framework deals with the three Cs of data literacy and the other can be used to develop and grow in your data literacy journey. These frameworks are designed to be modified and made your own.

The Three Cs Data Literacy Framework

The framework for the three Cs of data literacy (curiosity, creativity, critical thinking) can strengthen your cognitive muscles. Let's see how we can use each of these on a daily basis for success.

CURIOSITY

The first C is curiosity and should take form by asking questions. Now, when should you ask questions? When you read something new or there is a data point you have discovered, instead of just taking it at face value, ask at least one question about it. For example, let's say you read a study on a new medicine that shows signs of improving XYZ health condition. How long did they study this medicine? How many patients saw the improvement versus those who didn't? Were there any side effects that could deter one from using the medicine? When will this be available?

Now, who is the greatest data literacy detective of all? It is children. Don't believe me? Sit with kids and see how many questions they ask, regularly. I have five kids, so how many questions do you think I get regularly? It is a lot. But you know what, they are figuring things out. They are learning. They are developing knowledge. If you are in your career, jump in and ask as many questions as you can, all over the organization. Learn from leaders and others, learn about data and analytics, learn about AI. Find answers and then ask more and more questions. Find more answers. Who knows, maybe you will find your "data literacy" moment, like I did, and propel your career forward.

Now, questions enhance your analytical skills when it comes to data. Questioning new data points doesn't mean it is inaccurate, but we want to foster curiosity. It may be that one question leads you down a path. If it is interesting to you, then follow it.

> TIP
>
> When you read something new, ask at least one question. Make this a rule. Ask: "What did I read?" or "How does this apply to me, if at all?" Asking questions can empower you in your career.

CREATIVITY

Now, what does creativity have to do with data literacy work? Well, in school, you may have found math, statistics, and data boring. So, we need to bring the human element to the data. If you are working with some data and visualizing it, maybe you can present it in a new way. If you are telling a data story, bring it to life and instead of just reciting the data, find a relatable example that embeds it in real life.

For example, imagine you want to bring a new product to market and think it could be a good addition to your organization's portfolio. Imagine if you just tell people the specifications of the product. That may not get people excited, but what if you approached it differently? What if you told a story about how the product is used in the home, or about how it has the power to transform a human experience? By relating to a person's life, the product comes to life. When Steve Jobs released the iPod and he had people dancing in its commercial, he didn't just give us the device specifications; it became about having your music in your pocket. We can sit and just use data points, or we can be creative and bring data to life in stories. Be creative.

TIP

Try to find at least one way to be creative with your data points. Find ways to be creative in your career. Is it a new visualization? A new story to tell? Find at least one way to be creative in all that you do with data.

CRITICAL THINKING

Time to flex those thinking muscles. Data is powerful when used appropriately. The reality is, though, data can be misused for agendas and to tell narratives that influence. Look at politics: how many misused data points exist there? Does that mean we shouldn't trust data? No, it doesn't. Instead, it means that when we find data points that come to us, instead of just believing them, we ask questions and critically think about them.

Critically thinking about data brings in both curiosity (with questions) and creativity (with new ways to think about things). So, how can you work out your critical thinking skills? As I learned from Cal Newport in the book *Deep Work*, shut off distractions.[3] Block off your calendar once a day for deep thinking, ignoring your phone, email, Slack, or Teams messages.

TIP

Block off 30 minutes per day to do critical thinking. This could be to read an article and ask questions. This could be studying and thinking about what you studied. Find things to critically think on and reflect. This could be a work project or problem you are working on. Also, don't forget to take notes and write down ideas.

The Data Literacy Framework

The Data Literacy Framework, similar to the Data and AI Confidence Framework in Chapter 2, provides a step-by-step approach to how you can develop and grow your data literacy skills. Remember the four characteristics of data literacy: reading, working with, analyzing, and communicating with data. There are different things you can learn in each, so remember to go about this strategically and don't take on too much. Make this a continual progression for yourself. Find the areas within these characteristics that you enjoy and learn more and more.

PRE-FRAMEWORK: ASSESSMENT

One thing that you can do to help you utilize this framework and develop more confidence in your data literacy journey is to take an assessment. This will provide you with an idea of where your skills are strong and where you may have gaps. So, before using the framework, find an assessment to take—asking a search engine or AI can be helpful to find one. Some of these assessments may cost money, but don't let that deter you. We should invest in ourselves to increase our confidence in data and AI.

After the assessment, you now can have your personal landscape of data and analytics skills and can move forward in growing these. Also, you can ask AI to help you understand the roadmap, framework, and how to close the skills gaps you have.

STEP 1: DETERMINE YOUR DESIRED OUTCOME

The first thing to do is to pick a topic. Think about what you want to learn, considering the results of your assessment. Apply this target specifically to the four characteristics: do you want to get better at reading data? Maybe you want to get better at your communication and find how to craft data stories and add data points to it.

Now, you can utilize your curiosity and critical thinking skills to dive in.

STEP 2: CREATE A STRATEGY TO ACCOMPLISH YOUR OUTCOME

The second thing you want to do is to create a strategy and roadmap that will get you to your desired outcome.

In Chapter 2, we spoke about the book *Legacy* by James Kerr, which states that the better the structure, the better the strategy.[4] The weaker the structure, the weaker the strategy. This can be applied to data literacy. To accomplish the outcome, make sure you are building a roadmap. Create milestones to hit through your journey. When you hit milestones, reward yourself.

Now, does the strategy and roadmap have to be long? No, your journey could actually be pretty short; but remember, you aren't done when you finish that one. You can start working toward a new outcome to achieve.

STEP 3: CREATE A ROUTINE AND ENVIRONMENT

Something you can do to help you on this journey is to find a routine that works for you for your learning.

Being consistently good can empower you on your journey to success. But, one key thing to note with your routine is don't be so rigid that you burn out or don't take time off if you need it. For example, if you aren't feeling well and push through with an early morning wake-up, you may be hindering your health and therefore it will take longer to get back to your routine.

STEP 4: CHOOSE YOUR LEARNING SOURCE

There are different learning sources available to help you with your data literacy journey. Do you like to watch YouTube videos for your learning? Are you a fan of podcasts? Do you like books (maybe you could buy my other books too, I wouldn't mind!) Do you like articles? Online training? There are various channels and opportunities for learning, so find the ones you enjoy so you are more likely to keep learning. Search engines like Google as well as generative AI can further help you discover the sources of learning to help you thrive with your data literacy journey.

Then take notes as you learn. These can be written notes or voice notes. Journaling can help you remember things you have studied and offer a place to return to your notes. Another example of why journaling is advantageous is because you can record questions, ideas, or thoughts that pop into your head. Don't miss the chance to study and/or experiment because you didn't write down the thought.

STEP 5: EXECUTE YOUR STRATEGY

Next, you need to actually get going on your journey. Once you have built your strategy, actually execute it and move forward.

One thing I don't want us to fall into is "New Year's Resolution Syndrome." How many people set New Year's resolutions and then fail with them? Why is it that they fail? Is it because they don't want to accomplish that goal and task? I am not sure that's the case. It is more likely that their strategy and structure weren't strong enough. Did they not have a roadmap? Did they not reward themselves as they progress? Don't let your data literacy journey fall into New Year's Resolution Syndrome.

To test whether your strategy has worked, it is useful to take the assessment you did at the beginning of this process again and see if you have improved.

STEP 6: ITERATE AND START AGAIN

The final step in the journey is to iterate and start again; this is key to data and analytics work. Once we reach our first goal, we find a new topic, maybe something we came across during our previous research, or something that we are now working with in our job.

Conclusion

The world of data and analytics can be intimidating, especially if it wasn't your chosen profession. It can also be overwhelming, but you don't have to bite off more than you can chew. You may be more data literate than you know. One thing we want to do is develop your data literacy into your business skills. That's the power of data literacy: helping you to grow and thrive in your career. One key is to develop your confidence in the four characteristics of data literacy: reading, working with, analyzing, and communicating with data.

Make this journey to data literacy and confidence a success by focusing on and enjoying the ride. Don't think you will have arrived, but instead make it so you are continually learning throughout your life. Then, find joy in that journey.

KEY TAKEAWAYS

- Data literacy is for all, and is not just utilized in technical roles. Not everyone needs to be a data scientist or AI engineer, but everyone can develop skills with data.
- The data and AI driven train—data and AI can be helpful in finding information, insight, and intelligence, which help us make decisions and deliver outcomes.
- The four levels of analytics are: descriptive, diagnostic, predictive, and prescriptive. Not everyone needs to learn the ins and outs of each. Find your place within these.
- The definition of data literacy is the ability to read, work with, analyze, and communicate with data.
- The three Cs of data literacy are curiosity, creativity, and critical thinking. Don't lose track of your critical thinking skills; use them and build those muscles.
- Don't just use the data literacy framework; make it your own.

Notes

1 The University of Texas, Permian Basin. How Much Communication Is Nonverbal? online.utpb.edu/about-us/articles/communication/how-much-of-communication-is-nonverbal/ (archived at https://perma.cc/MM45-8WE5)

2 D. McRaney (2022) *How Minds Change: The Surprising Science of Belief, Opinion, and Persuasion*, Portfolio/Penguin, New York

3 C. Newport (2016) *Deep Work: Rules for Focused Success in a Distracted World*, Grand Central Publishing

4 J. Kerr (2013) *Legacy: What the All Blacks Can Teach Us About the Business of Life*, Constable & Robinson

4

AI and AI Literacy

Throughout history, some topics have gained a lot of buzz. For example, when the clocks turned from 1999 to 2000 there was a thing called "Y2K." Now, a topic garnering huge discussion is artificial intelligence (AI). Also, data literacy itself could be seen as a buzzword. The world of data and AI seems to be littered with buzz and hype. Navigating this when the majority of people are not data or AI professionals by background can be tricky, but this book will help you develop your skills and confidence so this becomes easier.

For the business world, AI's transformative power rivals that of the internet, the smartphone or personal computer, and automobiles. It may even go beyond rivalling these technologies because it can be very impactful and transformative to the technologies themselves. However, alongside this hype, AI has also brought a lot of uncertainty around how it will impact business operations and existing jobs.

This chapter will help you build more foundational knowledge about AI to improve your AI literacy and therefore your confidence, whilst navigating this rapidly evolving area. Do not fear it, embrace it and find how you can utilize it as your partner and friend. Remember, everyone has a seat at the AI table.

Generative AI and the World Today

Let us first discuss what was a big catalyst for all this hype: in November 2022, ChatGPT, a widely used form of generative AI, was launched.[1] This helped the world to embark on the journey of generative AI (GenAI). GenAI can be defined as "artificial intelligence ... that can create original content—such as text, images, video, audio or software code—in response to a user's prompt or request."[2]

The type of model that powers generative AI is called a large language model (LLM). These are "a category of foundation models trained on immense amounts of data making them capable of understanding and generating natural language and other types of content to perform a wide range of tasks."[3] LLMs can make our lives easier by, following an input (prompt), providing responses that we can utilize for decision making, learning, and/or idea generation.

Now, let us look at some real-world use cases where generative AI is being used today.

Healthcare[4]

AI is becoming more empowered to help society through healthcare. Some examples of how we are seeing generative AI help in health care are:[5]

- being "twice as accurate" as professionals at assessing stroke victims' brain scans
- detecting a higher number of bone fractures than doctors can
- detecting the presence of specific diseases before the patient experiences any symptoms

Through the improvements listed above, AI has the potential to create better medicines to tackle some of the world's most dangerous illnesses.

Advertising and Marketing[6]

The creation of ideas and content is one of the main activities in advertising and marketing. Utilizing AI provides a great opportunity to get help with the following activities:

- producing marketing text and images

- creating personalized recommendations for customers
- writing content such as product descriptions
- improving search engine optimization

Manufacturing[7]

Now, manufacturing may have more hands-on work than other areas, so people may be less aware of AI's impact in this context, but let us show you some examples. AI is very helpful in creating solutions in the manufacturing sector. It can aid in:

- Improving the speed of the design process.
- Delivering smart maintenance solutions for heavy equipment. For example, one time my dishwashers had an issue. Instead of having to explore and look around, the person who we hired to fix it plugged in a computer or device and it helped me solve the issue. We were then able to fix the dishwashers.
- Enhancing supply chain processes, by helping predict supply chain needs or helping create supply chain strategies.

Sales

In the world of sales, the ability to build relationships is key to empower sales and expansions. This can be from helping build sales strategies with AI for existing customers or by using AI to analyze a market or potential client. AI can help do the following:

- Create tailored, creative, and powerful communications to clients.
- Empower innovative idea generation to overcome challenges and roadblocks to success.
- Give ideas about negotiations—do you like negotiation? Some people do, and others probably don't. That is okay, allow AI to give you ideas to help you succeed with negotiations.
- Understand market trends and carry out research—allow it to be your PhD partner to help you thrive with learning and growth.

AI Agents

AI agents are a type of agentic AI. AI agents are defined as: "a system or program that is capable of autonomously performing tasks on behalf of a user or another system by designing its workflow and utilizing available tools."[8] We need to remember that AI agents can be enhanced by generative AI models (including large language models). This could be for defining and running a collections process, for example. In a collections process for a bill that is unpaid, the AI agent could send out automated emails for those bills that have gone delinquent.

AI agents are being used in multiple industries. For example, in sales and marketing, AI sales agents build lead lists, send personalized communications, and analyze competitor activities. In customer support, these agents take actions on behalf of users, recommend products, or handle more complicated technical support issues.[9, 10]

Let us look at some examples of AI agents:[11]

- **Simple reflex agent:** These are the most basic type of AI agent. These are agents that make a decision based primarily on their current perceptions and follow specific rules which govern their behavior. For example, an automatic door sensor is a simple reflex agent: when it senses movement, it opens the doors.
- **Model-based reflex agent:** These agents are more advanced than simple reflex, building upon a model of the world, which helps them keep track of their environment. Think of Roomba vacuums: they are working with the model of a room and navigating it for their end purpose.
- **Goal-based agent:** This type of agent takes the simple reflex agent a bit further by incorporating a goal-oriented technique to problem-solving. Its ability to reason enables it to act with more foresight.
- **Utility based agent:** These agents are designed to achieve goals whilst maximizing utility. These are resource-intensive because they are more complex. One example would be autonomous driving cars.
- **Learning agent:** A learning agent learns over time, based on the new data and experience it has.

One useful thing you can do is learn how you can interact with the results of an AI agent. Learn how to ensure they are operating correctly and providing you with their benefits. Find pain points or tasks that take you a lot of time; if an AI agent can do this task, it frees your time for other issues or tasks.

AI Literacy

I say people have seats at the data and AI table, and they do. But what does that seat look like? Do you want to go back to school and learn how to develop machine learning or large language models? Probably not. That's not what is needed for the majority of people. Instead, the world of AI literacy enters.

With all types of generative AI, machine learning, and natural language processing, you may ask what your role is with these technologies. This is where the world of AI literacy steps in. Learning how to code or develop models isn't what you need to worry about. Like data literacy, AI literacy is here to empower the masses to be confident with AI.

AI literacy is the ability to prompt, evaluate, and make decisions with the AI response. Pretty straightforward, right? Let's break the definition down more for you and start by talking about prompting AI.

Prompting AI

Have you ever explored prompting AI? Have you used ChatGPT, Gemini, or Claude? An AI prompt is "an input or instruction given to an AI system to elicit a specific response or result. Prompts serve as a bridge between human intent and machine interpretation, allowing users to guide AI behavior and interaction."[12] The nice thing is, you can interact and prompt the AI like you are talking with another human. You don't have to use technical language or be an AI expert to prompt the AI and evaluate the response you receive.

There are different kinds of prompts, which are outlined here.

GENERATIVE PROMPT

A generative prompt is used to generate something for you, like an idea, story, or image. In a business setting, you may want an image for a presentation. You can prompt the AI to create it: "I am in need of an image of a person teaching a class, please create one." With this prompt, you will receive a generated image that you can use. If you don't like the image, you can push back and have it generate a new one, prompting what you would like it to change.

DESCRIPTIVE PROMPT

These types of prompts are used to get descriptive outputs, like summarizing information. For example, you may upload a PDF into a generative AI tool and ask it to summarize the PDF for you.

Imagine you receive a PDF of an earnings release: it is long, but you are crunched for time for a meeting. You can upload it to generative AI and then ask it to summarize so you can have the highlights from it for your meeting. You could use a prompt like this: "I am in a rush as an organization I am meeting with in the afternoon released its earnings report this morning. I don't have time to read all the pages; can you summarize the attached document and give me highlights? Thank you."

INSTRUCTIONAL PROMPT

This would be a prompt to elicit step-by-step instructions for something. Here is an example of an instructional prompt: "I have been put on a new project at work but because I have never done this work, I am a little worried I won't get it right. The project is to help build a new marketing campaign for a new product. Our marketing has been stale and old, we need to innovate. Can you help me create a roadmap for building this campaign? What information do you need from me?"

CONVERSATIONAL PROMPT

Think of this type of prompt as engaging a user, enhancing their experience, such as a chatbot for customer service.[13] Another example of using a conversational prompt could be a leader or procurement team visiting a site to learn about a product context: "Hi, I am visiting your site to learn about product XYZ. Could you please tell me about the product and how I can apply it to my organization?"

Prompting is something you should experiment with and try, perhaps to plan a vacation or create a workout plan, before working with it in your role. You can work within a generative AI model such as Gemini from Google or ChatGPT from OpenAI. Do note that responses can vary between repetitions of prompts, as these models build predictions based off of the prompt you give it. Essentially, the AI takes your prompt and utilizes the data it trained on to give you a predicted response to what you want. It is very good at this, so the response it gives you is often useful. However, you can always re-prompt—and remember, the more specific your prompt, the better the response.

Below is a prompt I put into Gemini, asking for career advice, and the response it provided.

> "With the world of AI advancing, I am worried. I don't have much experience with AI. I have only used it where it is embedded in a tool, like Alexa with Amazon. I work in sales and want to learn how to utilize AI to improve my career. What are some things I can do to help me with my AI skill set? Can you create for me a roadmap for learning and developing in AI?"

To summarize Gemini's response:

- It built out a Phase 1 foundational understanding. In this section it started by demystifying AI. That is a good place to start because if we don't know what something is and we try to use it, we will most likely use it incorrectly. Also, if we don't understand it, it can have limitations we don't know about. After demystifying AI, it went into personal application. Application is key because if we are looking to improve our AI skills, it doesn't help if we just think of theory.
- In Phase 2, it looked at AI in sales and professional development, listing sales-specific tools and areas for skills enhancement.

Enhancement of our work is key: AI should be a partner and not supersede us.

- In Phase 3, we looked to deepening knowledge and ethical considerations. This matters greatly because we want to use AI responsibly. We don't want to cause issues or lose someone's trust because we used it in a manner that isn't responsible.

Overall, the AI offered some helpful advice to become more confident. Adapt the prompt with your job role and career goals and see the roadmap AI provides you with.

The first portion of AI literacy is knowing how to prompt. Did my examples help you to think of new ways you could use generative AI in your career? Now, we need to evaluate the responses we receive so we may know that it is a good response.

Evaluating Prompts

When an AI model gives us a response, we need to ensure that the information it is giving us is accurate and usable. If it isn't, you can prompt it that the information isn't true or usable and to please generate a new response. But how can you determine if it provides value in the first place? Let's look at some ways:

READ THROUGH THE RESPONSE AND CRITICALLY THINK ABOUT IT

When AI gives us a response or information, we should be utilizing our cognitive muscles to read through the response and be critical. Think of our prompt above. Ensure you read through the prompt response and make sure it is logical and is relevant—has it provided the information you need, in the way that you asked for it? Furthermore, if in the prompt, you gave more specific details about your experience, ensure the response aligns with these details and makes sense overall.

Remember when using AI in your role, the response must be relevant to your role, the business, and the project you are working on to be implemented successfully.

CROSS-CHECK INFORMATION WITH SOURCES

To validate AI you may actually need to research some of the responses, or you may ask the AI to give you the sources that it used, if it didn't already. You should be aware that AI can make things up or hallucinate. AI hallucinations are phenomena wherein a large language model (LLM) perceives patterns or objects that are nonexistent or imperceptible to human observers and creates outputs that are nonsensical or altogether inaccurate.[14]

Essentially, AI can make things up. We need to ensure we spot this and, if inaccurate, avoid using that information for our business decisions.

Let us look at a few examples of AI hallucinations.[15]

- A widely used chatbot was asked in 2023 for an overview of a new scientific study, but generated details about the experiments that did not exist. Why does this matter? Because if you start to run ahead with "scientific evidence" and don't realize the data is false, you can share information that is incorrect. Then, if people make decisions based on that information, it can lead to poor outcomes.
- A summarization tool was used to condense a legal document. AI fabricated legal terms and also left out crucial details, which resulted in a summary that misrepresented the original document. This can have far-reaching negative implications for businesses and the stakeholders involved.
- AI systems can be used in the medical space to analyze x-rays, which is a great addition to our lives. In this case, it was designed to diagnose a certain medical condition. However, it did not identify the issue, and instead created a condition that wasn't found in the patient's medical history. This obviously poses a huge problem, so highlights the need to evaluate the prompt response carefully.

Yes, AI hallucinations happen. Should that stop us from using AI? No, because we will take the time to evaluate the responses given to us. Our goal is to evaluate the prompt responses and ensure we are receiving good answers and responses we can utilize effectively and safely.

HAVE SOMEONE DOUBLE-CHECK YOUR WORK

Another way to evaluate the work is to get someone else's opinion on the output. If you aren't sure how to view some data and information, why not reach out to people you know and get their thoughts? Utilize friends and colleagues to help you with determining the legitimacy of AI's outputs. Another way this helps is that another person may possess IQ and EQ that we do not have. So, they are able to bring their human elements to the table and help with understanding the AI response. We will discuss IQ and EQ more later in the book.

Don't just prompt an AI and then take the response as fact. The key to evaluating a prompt is to critically think about it and ask questions about it. We don't want to lose our cognitive muscles when we start to rely on AI more and more. Instead, allow AI to complement and support human intelligence.

Executing Decisions with Prompt Responses

The final part of AI literacy is knowing how to use the results from an AI prompt to make decisions and execute them. Now, let's make sure we are clear: not every prompt requires a big, long decision-making process. Sometimes, we are just asking a quick question about an AI topic. So, how can we execute decisions from generative AI outputs?

First, consider what your intention was with your prompt in the first place. If you are looking to plan a vacation, your intention is to use the itinerary it comes up with. You could then establish a budget and book the hotels and flights.

Let's ask a question: when you receive information to make a decision, such as what the weather will be like tomorrow, and you know you have a sporting event to attend, how do you react and make a decision with that information? It may absolutely come naturally to you. Well, let's make it the same with AI. At a conference I once attended, it was said to not view or think of AI as a tool but as a partner.

A Day in Your Life with AI

Now, we have been talking a lot about generative AI, but please remember it is not the only type of AI out there. For the majority of people, though, it will be the one utilized the most. Below are some examples of how to use generative AI in your day-to-day work.

Example 1: To Generate New Ideas

Have you ever been stuck on a work project? Maybe you feel like you aren't coming up with any new or revolutionary idea to bring the project forward. Go ahead and ask AI. Make sure the prompt is detailed to ensure you get a good outcome. Ask it to give you a strategy and structured roadmap. Let it be a partner for you on your work on this project.

> TIP
>
> Do remember, though, that when you utilize generative AI we want to ensure that any sensitive information we input cannot be used to train the model. You can research how to protect personal and company data in these models and turn off the training function. That way, you are in a position to input information that you don't want getting out into the public domain.

Example 2: Improving, Understanding, and Expanding Strategies

In your career, have you ever had to build a strategy or been confused by a strategy? Use generative AI to help you improve, understand, or expand a strategy. How does it do this? By providing insight and information we may not have. Remember, AI can possess knowledge we don't, it can go through other strategies and pull out information we didn't have before. It is a good source to help us improve knowledge. Again, note here that you want to ensure you aren't putting your company strategy into a public generative AI model that may train on the information you provide it. Instead, ensure you have a private and secure generative AI you can upload a strategy to.

Example 3: Learning and Development

Using generative AI to learn about and understand a topic can be more effective than using a search engine like Google. What do I mean here? Imagine you want to develop understanding and knowledge on project management. This is a new area for you, but you want to develop skills around this topic so you can manage the workload you have.

You go into a generative AI model and feed it information about your role, your background, and that you want to develop knowledge and skills within project management. The AI then gives you a response, considering your work, your personality, and your skills. You can then prompt the AI to build a roadmap for your learning. You create milestones and then you implement the learnings and advice.

Overall, AI can be a helpful tutor for your personal development. Don't miss out on this key way to utilize generative AI to enhance your skills and talents at your company and in your career.

Using AI: A Framework

For you to effectively and confidently utilize AI, a framework may help, as the topic of AI can be overwhelming and having a guide may help to improve your abilities, and ultimately confidence, to succeed with the power of AI. The steps of the framework are as follows:

1. Determine your objective.
2. Find your AI partner of choice.
3. Craft your prompt.
4. Prompt the AI solution.
5. Evaluate the prompt response.

6 Iterate or expand the prompt, if necessary, for better responses.
7 Make a decision on the prompt response, if needed.
8 Start anew.

1: Determine Your Objective

What are you looking to accomplish with a prompt? Now, for this framework, you may prompt something for a simple reply, or you may need to go deeper. Either way is great. Knowing your objective will help you to not get distracted and will empower you to drive more effective work with generative AI.

With your objective in hand, you are ready for step 2.

2: Find Your AI Partner of Choice

Now, you may already have a generative AI partner of choice, like ChatGPT or Gemini. I am not going to prescribe which tool to use. Instead, I suggest that you test out various tools and determine which one you like. You can test multiple solutions if you want to and then start to use it.

How can testing multiple solutions help? By utilizing different AI tools to determine which you like, you may find one easier to use than another, or that you prefer the responses that come from one. Now let's move on to step 3.

3: Craft Your Prompt

Okay, you need to now craft your prompt. Don't be ambiguous with your prompts; add specific details in even if it seems silly.

Ensure you tell the generative AI what you are looking for, if applicable. Also tell the AI solution what you want the response to look like. If you want it to give you a step-by-step program, tell it. If you want it to give you an outline or list, let it know. With your prompt, you can be specific and have it operate in ways you prefer and get the outcomes you are looking for. Make this about you and your personality. If there are details that you feel will help the AI deliver a good response to you, then add them in. You can always alter the prompt and iterate again if you want.

4: Prompt the AI Solution

The next step is simple: put the prompt in and let it give you a response.

5: Evaluate the Prompt Response

The next step is to evaluate the prompt response that the AI solution gives you. You should develop and use your critical thinking skills to ensure the prompt makes sense, is valid, and gives you the response you want. Don't just start using the response, read through it and study it. One key thing you can do to ensure the prompt response is accurate is to question it. Ask questions like:

- Does this response tie back to what I was looking for?
- Why did it respond this way and is it following the instructions I gave it?
- Can the AI provide the sources it has cited?
- If I use my intuition and thoughts, does it make sense? (However, remember that our intuition and thoughts can be wrong.)
- Is there a better way to prompt this to get a better response?

TIP

Make sure you are flexible and not stuck in having to how you want the AI to respond to you. In this case, we are expecting or wanting the prompt responses to be a certain way. Instead, be open to different. What I mean is the AI might teach you something you weren't expecting, and that is okay. Be open to the new and the art of the possible, as the AI may empower you along the way.

Another thing you can do is to cross-check the prompt response about known things. If you are trying to make a recipe for chocolate chip cookies and it leaves sugar or chocolate out of the recipe, you would question what the recipe is doing. In a business setting, if you are trying to generate a communication for a client about a new offering coming up and the communication created by the AI mentions the wrong client name or does not provide the key information, then you should go back in. Re-prompt the AI and let it know where it went wrong. Then, generate a new response.

We can't have our cognitive muscles weaken because we are relying too much on AI, so use it as your partner and not something that supersedes human intelligence.

6: Iterate or Expand the Prompt, If Necessary, for Better Responses

Don't let AI be a one-stop shop, prompting it once, taking the response, and moving on. No, as you critically think about the response and move forward, ensure you are iterating your prompt. Test it out and see if you can improve the prompt for a better response. If we return to the previous example about generating a communication with a client about a new offering, what if the response did not convey the excitement about the new offering? Don't just go with it. Push against the AI and challenge it to be better. Ask it to enhance a section or sentence or adapt the tone. Don't just prompt and turn your brain off. Allow yourself to combine with the AI and get a better response, if needed and/or desired.

What if the prompt response gives you some information that isn't close to what you need? That is okay, too. Instead of worrying, go back to your prompt and see if you can figure out why it didn't work the way you wanted. Then, re-prompt the AI and move forward with the new response. You can experiment and test it. Give the AI model feedback in the form of a prompt to share that it either worked or didn't work.

Keep the prompting going to help you get results that are in line with the needs of the business if applying AI to your role, or what you like and what you want to see, if you're using AI to enhance your skills for career progression.

7: Make a Decision on the Prompt Response, if Needed

If you are looking to utilize the prompt response for a decision, then act upon it. Don't get caught up in an "I don't know" mentality, unless it may be beneficial to delay, or it is a big decision that needs input from multiple stakeholders.

If you have critically thought about the decision, then you can move forward with it. I recommend documenting your decision by writing it down. This is so you do not forget your thought processes and you can learn from them. Furthermore, if the AI leads to a helpful decision, your document can be referred back to, either by you or other members of your team.

Then, evaluate the output: what happened after you made the decision? As you make more useful and successful decisions with AI, you are able to gain more confidence.

8: Start Anew

Now that you have gone through the previous seven steps, you can start anew. Start to make it a part of who you are and how you do things, where appropriate. Start to utilize AI in your job in an effective manner to improve your creativity. AI can help your creativity in business settings in numerous ways, such as making emails more creative, starting a new type of marketing campaign, or creating a whole new way of delivering a public speaking session.

Conclusion

Do not fear AI—there are many ways to incorporate these different solutions into your life. AI literacy does not mean developing technical knowledge. We want you to use AI in an effective manner. Literacy can empower you to use it effectively within your sphere of work, from prompting it well to evaluating the prompt and making decisions with its outputs. Feel empowered and confident as you work.

KEY TAKEAWAYS

- AI is empowering the world in different ways.
- AI literacy is the ability to prompt, evaluate the prompt, and make decisions with the AI.
- Hallucinations happen, but you can evaluate the response and find where the incorrect information is.
- Be empowered by an AI framework, but make it your own.

Notes

1 A. Heienickle. ChatGPT Timeline: The Evolution of AI-Powered Conversations, ADOGY, May 21, 2025, www.adogy.com/chatgpt-timeline-the-evolution-of-ai-powered-conversations/ (archived at https://perma.cc/ZY2H-9CCQ)

2 M. Scapicchio and C. Stryker. What Is Generative AI?, IBM, March 22, 2024, www.ibm.com/think/topics/generative-ai (archived at https://perma.cc/VJ8Y-MHHA)

3 IBM. What Are Large Language Models (LLMs)? November 2, 2023, www.ibm.com/think/topics/large-language-models (archived at https://perma.cc/Y5BC-ESWF)

4 Coursera Staff. 20 Examples of Generative AI Applications Across Industries, June 3, 2025, www.coursera.org/articles/generative-ai-applications (archived at https://perma.cc/AN87-R8F4)

5 World Economic Forum. 7 Ways AI Is Transforming Healthcare, World Economic Forum, August 13, 2025, www.weforum.org/stories/2025/08/ai-transforming-global-health/ (archived at https://perma.cc/X8LJ-2REX)

6 Coursera Staff. 20 Examples of Generative AI Applications Across Industries, June 3, 2025, www.coursera.org/articles/generative-ai-applications (archived at https://perma.cc/H54A-F4YJ)

7 Coursera Staff. 20 Examples of Generative AI Applications Across Industries, June 3, 2025, www.coursera.org/articles/generative-ai-applications (archived at https://perma.cc/H54A-F4YJ)

8 A. Gutowska. What Are AI Agents? IBM, www.ibm.com/think/topics/ai-agents (archived at https://perma.cc/AF87-92K4)

9 M. Nagpal. 7 Types of AI Agents with Examples and Use Cases, ProjectPro, November 14, 2024, www.projectpro.io/article/types-of-ai-agents/1066 (archived at https://perma.cc/RTW7-MB4H)

10 I. Ism. 11 Real-World AI Agent Examples in 2025, Chatbase, October 28, 2024, www.chatbase.co/blog/ai-agent-examples (archived at https://perma.cc/2KCH-UJS9)

11 C. Stryker. Types of AI Agents, IBM, www.ibm.com/think/topics/ai-agent-types (archived at https://perma.cc/6G58-NY5R)

12 MEFMobile. Guide to AI Prompts: What They Are and How to Write Them, January 4, 2025, mefmobile.org/guide-to-ai-prompts-what-they-are-and-how-to-write-them/ (archived at https://perma.cc/7VNG-CKS5)

13 MEFMobile. Guide to AI Prompts: What They Are and How to Write Them, January 4, 2025, mefmobile.org/guide-to-ai-prompts-what-they-are-and-how-to-write-them/ (archived at https://perma.cc/7VNG-CKS5)

14 IBM. What Are AI Hallucinations? September 1, 2023, www.ibm.com/think/topics/ai-hallucinations (archived at https://perma.cc/5YB3-BF74)

15 A. Khan. AI Hallucinations Examples: Top 5 and Why They Matter, Lettria, October 1, 2024, www.lettria.com/blogpost/top-5-examples-ai-hallucinations (archived at https://perma.cc/43RX-Z4JZ)

5

How to Build a Plan to Succeed with Data and AI

When we think of data and AI confidence, how do we build this within ourselves? Are you using data and AI in your job but feel overwhelmed? Are you unsure how you can use it effectively? Well, one thing that can help a person to develop confidence is a plan. Having a plan is a great way for us to dive in and progress to milestones and outcomes. Don't just take it on from guesswork. Instead, push toward success and drive toward an outcome. There are business examples of building plans or using data and AI to make solutions, but a relatable one may be a personal example. Let's use an everyday example of taking a vacation that will illustrate how you can use a plan to make a decision first, and then we can apply it to data and AI.

When I turned 40, I had the opportunity to go on a trip to Italy. Italy was such a wonderful place and somewhere I would go back to. I live across the ocean from Italy, so planning things can help to make this experience better and ensure that my wife and I have confidence that the trip will be pleasant. Our plan included certain days when we would go hit main tourist attractions, like the Colosseum and Vatican City, but we didn't make the plan too rigid so that we had freedom within the trip to do other things. For example, we had an open period of time in Florence, and I found a pizza and gelato making class and it turned out to be great. In fact, it was one of the best pizzas I have ever had.

What can we learn from planning a vacation that we can take into the world of building a plan for data and AI? Let's take a look at a few things:

- **Experiencing the unknown**—I can read and learn about Italy but until I go there, I will never truly "know" it in an experiential way. Similarly, we can read and learn about data and AI, but until we experience it, it isn't going to have an impact in our own lives. We can experience AI by utilizing a tool like ChatGPT or Gemini, through a company's chatbot that helps customers, or even through predictive analytics that help us make decisions. If you find yourself stumped on how data and AI are going to help you to make the decisions, to find the applicability, then dive into AI and ask it: "How will this help me make a decision?" or "How will this drive value?"
- **Leave time to experiment**—When my wife and I traveled to Italy, we left time to explore. For some of the days, we had a planned activity, but then we had free time. How can we apply this to a plan for data and AI? Well, we don't want to bog our plan down and not allow for flexibility, as this can cause ourselves unnecessary frustration and stress. Now, in this case, become like a kid again, as they are the best data literacy detectives. Don't forget that curiosity or creativity. Use them to your advantage and experiment.
- **Prepare for your learning**—While our Italy trip had room for experimentation, we also planned ahead. We found flights that worked, we coordinated with another couple that joined us on the trip, and we found enjoyable activities. Ensure you are preparing ahead for your learning and work with data and AI. Maybe there is a topic you are looking to study but then you don't research the sub-topics to include in your plan, meaning the plan will be more haphazard and frustrating.
- **Keep your eyes open**—On our trip we traveled to the city of Bolzano in the Dolomites mountains. I didn't realize a company I liked, Salewa, was headquartered in this city. The way I discovered Salewa originally was on a different trip with my wife to Barcelona.

So, we visited the Bolzano store, and I was able to buy some things I liked. This was a reminder that if we don't have our eyes open for our plans, we may miss things that are interesting or fun. Keep your eyes open with data and AI. There may be areas that would interest you but if you aren't open to possibilities, you may miss them.

Having now understood the basis of planning, let me share what this chapter will cover. We will first cover what success looks like with data and AI. We will also look at what the term "confidence" means (hint, it won't mean you know everything). Success can look different for different people, so let's help you establish what success could look like for you.

Next, we will cover the term "value" for data and AI. Like success, value can be different for different people. So, we want to help you start to derive value for yourself with data and AI. Again, you don't need to know everything but let's help you build a plan to create value in your career.

The third area we will cover in this chapter is hype vs. reality. What is real and what isn't? Finally, we will help you with building a plan for data and AI confidence. Let's jump into the sections.

Defining Success for Data and AI

It is key for everyone to understand that you don't need to be technical or have advanced knowledge to have confidence with data and AI. One thing you will want to do, though, is look at how you would define success with data and AI.

Success for data and AI derives from how we bring value from them into our careers. Look at the travel example above: how could we have determined whether we had derived value from our AI usage for a trip to Italy? It could be if we were able to effectively and efficiently plan the vacation with more ease, saving time and energy. However, we do need to allow grace and flexibility when working with AI. What if you used AI to help plan the entire trip, only to find the suggestions it gave weren't what you had hoped they would be? Maybe a couple of outings weren't up to your liking, so those didn't help you have the most fun on your trip. From here, you may think that AI wasn't successful, but does the AI not giving you the recommendations you were hoping for mean it was unsuccessful?

Don't view data and AI as having to be perfect in order for you to have confidence and gain success with it. We don't need to be perfect, but the better our AI literacy is, like how we prompt it, can help us achieve results we are more likely to utilize.

Overall, value can be defined in multiple ways:

Learning Opportunities

Learning is a wonderful determinant of value when we are trying to build skills and confidence with data and AI. How many books have you read? How many courses are you taking? Have you applied any theoretical knowledge to your work? Are we experimenting with data and AI, finding where it is working and not working, and documenting it so we can apply it in our roles?

A quote from Nelson Mandela, a personal hero, can help understand this concept: "I never lose. I either win or learn."[1] If not everything the AI response offered was successful and full of everything you had hoped, that is okay. Instead of looking at it as a failure, view it as a learning opportunity. Therefore, one key thing to help you define success with data and AI is asking whether you learnt something from the journey you took.

Change

You can measure value by seeing and observing the change driven by data and AI usage. Using data and AI in your life to make decisions and drive outcomes can lead to positive changes, such as higher productivity. For me, I use a deep research function within Gemini by Google to write whitepaper-type reports for me on topics I am learning. Another example from my career was when I had to improve a report building process. For my organization, we had an Excel file that was used to track our publicly traded clients. This was a manual process. I took the time to build an LLM model that trained on the documentation of our publicly traded clients. Then, the teams could just prompt the LLM model for questions about publicly traded clients. No need to build the manual Excel file any more. The end users could just use the LLM model that was built.

Below are some examples of deriving value from AI and data that could bring about value from learning opportunities and/or change:

- Utilizing a prompt that helps to create and drive a new marketing campaign. This is one way you can utilize AI to help improve upon the marketing campaign and ideas you have had in the past. In fact, it is a way to generate new ideas, new thoughts, and drive forward with stronger perspective. Then, you have the ability to evaluate the prompt response to build an effective campaign. Ask yourself: how can I iterate upon this to improve the work I am doing? Did it capture enough for me? Did I utilize it to drive innovation and make it impactful?
- Utilizing AI as a tutor to help you learn; these learnings can then be applied elsewhere. Have you tried this yet? Have you created a study plan? What if you are trying to increase your leadership skills and want to build custom training for you where you have a skills gap? You can utilize AI to drive your leadership skills and learning. If you are brand new in your career, you can have AI craft an assessment for you and find your skills gaps. Then, you can use these results to help you build competencies in leadership learning.
- Using data to understand a client and its needs. By learning about the client more, we can make more customized recommendations or work for them instead of general work. Then, we can utilize AI for idea generation around the data we have studied. Hopefully, this empowers the client to trust you more as you are not just giving generalities but specific and customized work.

The Three Is

As outlined in Chapter 3, success with data and AI can be boiled down to my three Is: information, insight, and intelligence. These three Is play a role in how you can define success with data and AI in your life.

INFORMATION

Our ability to derive information from data and AI models and insights is important, as the information we find and how we use it can determine success. Is the information accurate? Have we evaluated it to determine whether it aligns with how we want to use it? Information can give us the "what," and sometimes with data and AI, information is all we need. A quick answer. For instance, "What does the weather look like today, and how should I dress to be comfortable in that weather?" is a data-informed decision. Instead of having to read multiple books or articles, you can turn to an AI tool to help you understand and learn things. New information can help you feel successful.

Now, sometimes in your data and AI driven work, in your work driving Engineered Intelligence, you don't need more than information and that is fine. Not all decisions are going to be long processes. In fact, a lot of times you will only need the short answer. Develop skills to determine when you need just information or when you need more.

INSIGHT

Insight is a "why" determination. With data and AI, we often need to know the "why" behind information. Let's say you work in marketing. You gather information from the data on a marketing campaign and discover the data shows the marketing campaign failed. That is good information to have. You know it failed, so you can determine not to do that type of campaign again. It may have been due to only one small part of the campaign that struggled. So, instead of re-doing the whole campaign, you shift one piece of it, and it performs better. You now are using data and AI to learn the "why" and improve your work.

Getting good and figuring out the insight within the data and AI may be one of the most important skills one can develop. Understanding the "why" behind things in the data is a powerful thing for individuals to understand. I will caution, though, that finding a direct "why" or insight can be hard. At times we are just looking at theories around "why" something happened. Then we can test.

One thing to remember is that just because things are correlated or look to be related, that doesn't mean one thing caused the other: correlation doesn't mean causation. This is a big reason to understand why you can experiment and test. Then, as more information comes through, you can keep testing, iterating, and discovering more insight.

INTELLIGENCE

The third "I" is intelligence. This is the integration of AI into your workflow. AI can help to provide you with more and/or new information and insight at rapid speed. Therefore, allowing AI to be a tutor and partner can be very beneficial. Remember, AI is unemotional and able to provide intelligence on many topics. With this in mind, as you prompt AI to bring intelligence to you, evaluate it, compare it, and ensure that it is correct.

These three Is are a way to help you define value from data and AI in your career. If you can derive information, insight, and/or intelligence from data and AI, those things can drive decisions and outcomes. This can empower you with more success from data and AI.

Data and AI: Hype vs. Reality

Within the world of data and AI, there is a lot of hype and bluster. Have you ever seen movies like *The Terminator*, *I, Robot*, or *Ex Machina*? The world is going to end with AI, right? Well, maybe not, but we should be cautious and optimistic at the same time. Instead of focusing on the hype, dystopia, or whatever negative ideas are out there, focusing on what we can and can't do with data and AI can help us to bring possibilities to life for ourselves. The art of the possible is a good thing and should be utilized, but thinking big is a powerful thing in our lives.

For example, you may have already heard the idea that AI agents can take over and do the work for us, resulting in widespread job loss. There is some truth to this for more manual roles, let's be clear, but it does not mean AI agents should or will take over everything. I am not worrying about the AI robot overlords taking over everything on us yet. There is still a long way to go before they will independently provide the value that humans can.

There are multiple ways to recognize instances of AI being hyped. Broad statements saying that it will "completely revolutionize" a particular industry is one such way.[2] Also, saying that it will solve all your problems or create all the necessary things for you to succeed is hyped-up talk that won't necessarily come to fruition.

Now, there is hype that can be viewed in a positive light. A lot of us are affected by cancer. I for one would love to see AI empower our healthcare and create better treatments for us, but I am not sure that AI will completely change anything, at least not by tomorrow. AI is more likely to support human thought, helping to empower us and be more effective and efficient in the spaces we work in. AI can be the partner that helps us to engineer intelligence. Remember our formula—it is the combination of the data and AI and the human elements of IQ and EQ. We can then augment ourselves, the human, and be empowered to make more intelligent decisions.

How Do We Overcome Hype and Base Our Work in Reality?

Key to understanding the hype vs. reality work in our lives is to not focus on the technology and the buzz it generates, but to focus strongly on use cases in our lives where it could be good for us to utilize AI as our partner. If we want to develop confidence with data and AI, we need to ensure that we are finding the right areas of our lives to help us achieve success with them. Here are some steps to do that.

STEP 1: EVALUATION OF PROBLEMS, PAINS, AND NEEDS

The first step to help you gain more confidence in utilizing data and AI effectively in your career is to evaluate different areas to see if data and AI are in a position to alleviate and help with problems, pains, and needs. For example, a need could be making a personal development plan for yourself and creating career ladders you can climb for success. Evaluating this need can be done through data, such as identifying your skill gaps.

Now, AI can help us to not just understand it internally but help us evaluate external factors, and trends, giving a more complete picture of the problem or pain point we are solving. For example, you can prompt generative AI and ask it for current trends within a certain industry that can empower you in marketing, with clients, or wherever it can empower you. You can ask it to predict future trends and ask it why it predicted them that way. This enables you to drive forward with strong building of knowledge and learning around various topics.

STEP 2: SELECT THE RIGHT TOOL OR TECHNOLOGY PARTNER

The second step to help you get through the hype and buzz is to effectively find the right tool or technology partner to help you with your problem, pain, or need. For me with learning, it is Deep Research from Gemini Google. When you are evaluating technology, remember it is advancing, and so you may need to set aside regular time to study and learn what's happening now.

You can determine which technology works for your problem, pain, or need simply through search engines or by asking AI.

STEP 3: UTILIZE THE PARTNER

For the problem, pain, or need you are looking to solve, you need to experiment and work with the technology partner to ensure it is solving what you want it to. So, take the time to experiment, learn what works, iterate, and refine. Then, you keep on going. What do you do if the partner doesn't work the way you want? That is okay, find a new partner and experiment.

STEP 4: EVALUATE THE OUTPUT

Key to ensuring the partner is working for you is to evaluate the output. You dig into the output and ensure it is giving you what you want to solve the problem. Now, one thing to be aware of is that the partner may not give you the exact solution you were looking for, but have an open mind that the result you were given could be utilized in a different way. Or, you could be provided with different ideas, which could spark further creativity.

STEP 5: EXECUTE YOUR DECISION

If your problem, pain, or need has a solution then you can implement it. Then, you can learn, pivot, and iterate. It is key to execute what you are looking to do. Why would you use data and/or AI as a partner if you weren't going to execute on the results? As you do, keep an open mind about the changing technology. As you continue to follow these steps, you can develop your data and AI confidence.

STUDYING AND LEARNING

One thing that wasn't listed in those steps is studying and learning. The knowledge we gain will help us to be more intelligent with data and AI, finding new ways to be creative and new ways to understand how to utilize the tools and technologies that now sit at our fingertips. We can utilize the power of our knowledge to grow and then apply to data and AI.

You may ask: "What learning matters?" Here, I think it is important to note that we aren't only talking about data and AI knowledge, but general knowledge overall. For example, it may be that you study the philosophy of Taoism or how ancient people thought and worked. You then use that information to think and understand how to apply things in the data and AI work you are taking on. You may find useful information and ways to improve your knowledge that then get applied to the work you are doing.

Utilize the Three Cs and Three Is

Now, let's discuss the three Cs and three Is of data and AI literacy. I devised the three Cs of data literacy a long time ago and they still matter today. We can now modify it to be the three Cs of data and AI literacy. Those three Cs are curiosity, creativity, and critical thinking, as introduced in Chapter 3. Now, how does this help with hype and buzz? Let's take a look.

CURIOSITY

When we are curious, we push conventional thinking, we ask questions. By asking questions, we can develop confidence as we learn new things and gain different perspectives. You may ask how it helps you to develop confidence. It does this by helping us gain understanding and knowledge of the tasks in front of us. When we are reading a headline, we can ask questions to the effect of: "How does this headline apply to me?" or "This is a pretty stark headline, I wonder if I dig in more there may be some more information that I can learn?" or "This doesn't make sense, I wonder if I am missing something?"

Questions can be a gateway to answers, and those answers may help us to sift through the buzz, the hype, the garbage, and help us to find the nugget of gold or insight that sits in front of us. This insight then can be utilized to further our careers, work, or even our lives.

CREATIVITY

The human skill of creativity is something we need to preserve in the midst of the hype of AI and we should not become over-reliant on the technology. Be creative, whether in your prompting or in your use of AI for problems, pains, or needs. An example of this is utilizing personal stories that people relate to and making the case for a solution to a business problem stronger. You can utilize your ideas, thoughts, experience, and put them into the prompt.

Now, it is one thing to just say "be creative" but you may then ask, how do I do that? You may even feel that you aren't creative. Like learning to ride a bike or drive a car, practice is going to matter for you here. Instead of just buying into the hype and fear, you creatively ask questions, you creatively apply the AI and technology in front of you, and you creatively work to understand the ins and outs where needed. Creativity can be working toward success and even working toward failure. Work to fail, to find the gaps, to find where the "hype" and "buzz" fall short. Then, work toward reality and use cases.

CRITICAL THINKING

Critical thinking can truly help us get past the buzz and hype, as we critically think on what we are reading and seeing. Utilize the power of curiosity to partner with critical thinking. You may read a headline, a book, or hear something on a podcast that alarms you. If you let it grow without critical thinking, it can grow like an illness that goes untreated. As we are working toward sound knowledge and understanding of the work and ideas around us, critical thinking on the information is like the medicine we need to overcome the hype and buzz.

The reality is, we need to not only critically think about buzz and hype, but also about the information we put into an AI system, the output and the tools themselves. We need to intelligently apply the tools and technologies in our careers, so we aren't caught up in hype but are rolling through with the effective use and partnership with them. We need to question the prompts we write and the responses the AI brings to us. We need to think critically about the tools we are using and if they are even the solution to use for the problem we are solving.

I want you to treat your thinking skills as a muscle. Like going to the gym and losing strength, like stopping running and losing endurance, without working on your critical thinking skills, they will weaken. We shouldn't lose that human element of critical thinking. An over-reliance on the AI can be the thing that weakens our cognitive muscles because we aren't working them out. Don't allow your cognitive muscles to atrophy. Use them, think about things, question them, and get beyond the hype.

One example of my career where critical thinking came into play was in the world of data literacy. As I was helping to invent and build data literacy early in my career, one thing started to come to life: organizations and people need a framework for data literacy. Had I not thought about this at all, I may not have been able to build the framework I did. The ability to think critically about and understand what trends are occurring and how do they apply to my career, my fields of study and work, and in my speaking engagements has been an ongoing task for me. You need to be able to critically think about what is happening.

REAL-WORLD EXAMPLE

In trying to determine a proof of concept (POC), I found an area of the business I was working at to test AI in. Using the RFP (request for proposal) process was very time consuming. Instead, I utilized AI to help decrease the time it took to respond to questions and we saw the efficiency increase.

If I didn't use my human intelligence to think about this as a potential POC, we may have thrown the AI tool against any problem and watched it fizzle and not succeed.

Your Personal Plan

Now, how do you develop your personal plan for success with data and AI? Well, my five-step plan can help you, but you need to ensure to use the three Cs of data and AI literacy and the three Is. You need to be a healthy data skeptic. You can also personalize the plan to make it your own.

Step 1: Determine Your Objective

The first step is you need to determine your objective. Your objective matters: what is it that you want to do? Do you want to learn to prompt well? Do you want to get better at analyzing data? Do you want to understand data principles more effectively? Do you just want to learn AI terminology? These are objectives. Please do not start with the technology. Start with what you want to accomplish.

An example we will use through all five steps is the following: imagine you are early in your career and want to develop a key skill to use data and AI effectively to empower your decision-making skills. So, the objective you have put in place is: "Develop skills to utilize data and AI to empower my decisions."

Step 2: Determine Your Strategy

The next step is to determine the strategy you will deploy to achieve your objective and make it effective and empowering. Don't just say "My strategy is to do X." Say "My strategy is to do X, and this is how I am going to do it…" Then, create milestones and a roadmap. Set aside time to ensure you have enough time scheduled to drive toward your goal and be disciplined.

Okay, turning back to our example. You want to develop skills to make better decisions using data and AI. What might your strategy look like? You can prompt AI to understand key skills you need, build an assessment, and ask AI to build a roadmap. You then add in the ability to add your human understanding, your personal data, as you progress through.

Step 3: Determine Your Tool to Empower Your Strategy and Objective

Now, to achieve your objective and strategy, you may need a tool to help you get there. Allow the objective and strategy to determine your tool and/or technology first—you do not want to start with the tool. Imagine building a house and you start with a hammer, but first you need a saw. Had you known the objective and strategy more effectively, you may have seen you needed the saw first. Then, make the technology a human-centered partner. You are the one driving this, not the technology.

In our example, you are looking to build skills to utilize data and AI to empower your decisions. What tools might you need? Do you have a generative AI tool at your disposal? Do you have access to data that can help you make smarter decisions and test decisions?

Step 4: Utilize the Right Skill Set

You need the right skills to succeed, because if you have set an objective that you don't have the skills to accomplish, you may grow frustrated. If you find that you don't have the right skills to achieve the strategy and objective, then learn these first. You can use the three Cs here to develop the skills.

Step 5: Create and Empower Your Environment

Your environment matters to ensure you are able to achieve what you want. Imagine you want to improve your diet, but your house is just stocked with the unhealthy food you love. This isn't going to help you achieve your goal. For me, I like to sit in the same spot on my couch in the early mornings before the day gets going. I can read, journal, and have that time for myself.

Finally, for you to accomplish your goal for data and AI driven skills for successful decision-making, being consistent can help you be successful. Do you have an environment that will help you succeed with data and AI driven decisions? Do you have an environment that will help study and prepare your skill set? If not, create the environment and go forward.

Conclusion

Overall, you can develop confidence by building a plan to develop your skills. Take the time to do it. There is hype and fear around data and AI, but the reality is that you can empower yourself to succeed. Don't get left behind: take hold of the opportunity and develop your success.

KEY TAKEAWAYS

- Remember to operate toward success and value; improve your skills to derive value from data and AI.
- Don't get caught up with the "shiny object," the thing that looks cool and fun. Instead, use the tool that is most appropriate for your use case.
- Craft your own personal plan for success.
- As you use data and AI, don't forget your own personal and human touch.

Notes

1 A. Herron. Remembering Nelson Mandela: "I Never Lose. I Either Win or Learn," *Indianapolis Recorder*, July 15, 2021, indianapolisrecorder.com/remembering-nelson-mandela-i-never-lose-i-either-win-or-learn (archived at https://perma.cc/7HRT-UQM2)

2 J. Daly. How to Spot AI Hype, AIhub, November 19, 2021, aihub.org/2021/11/19/how-to-spot-ai-hype/- (archived at https://perma.cc/U8T5-TB9T)

6

The Power of Data and AI Use Cases

In the last chapter we discussed the value of data and AI, evaluating problems and how to help you navigate the hype of AI with confidence. In this chapter, let's now take it a step further and dive into the world of use cases.

A use case can be defined as a way to utilize data and AI for a particular purpose. Now, you may ask: what do I mean by particular purpose? Look no further than the goals and objectives that your organization is trying to achieve. Not what you want from data and AI, but what your organization is trying to accomplish. So, for our purposes with data and AI, a use case is a particular way one could use data and AI to achieve something, like an increase in sales or marketing reach. An example of a data use case could be using data to study and understand a new and emerging market. For AI, a use case could be using an AI tool for building tailored communication for clients. You could even use AI to understand a new market and have it write training materials on that market for you.

As mentioned in the previous chapter, there is a lot of hype and buzz in the world of data and AI—perhaps more than any other I have seen in the business world except for maybe the internet when it was coming out! Unvalidated hype is not a good thing. It can cause misunderstanding, misuse, and unethical use. So, now I will give you a way to help you develop more confidence in data and AI, empowering you as you put the work in to learn these fields. In the business world, use cases can be a key component to doing work effectively because a business has many goals, objectives, and targets. Consider those as a way to determine use cases.

The aim of this chapter is to give you some examples of use cases with data and AI, providing ideas that you may be able to use and adapt in your career. This chapter will also provide two checklists: the first checklist covers how to pick good use cases, and the second describes how to deploy your use case.

Data Use Cases

Data Use Case 1: Starbucks

Our first use case comes from the famous coffee chain Starbucks. How many of you enjoy a cup of coffee during your day (or maybe a couple)? Starbucks is empowering itself by using data and artificial intelligence. Starbucks is able to capture the transactions for individual purchase data from its millions of customers through its mobile app and loyalty card program. This data enables them to predict purchases and even give individual offers through the app or email. It also harnesses the data from individuals if they haven't visited a Starbucks location recently, sending them a customized email.[1] Therefore, customizing user experiences can be a way a business harnesses data for a use case.

Data Use Case 2: Coca-Cola

Maybe you aren't a coffee drinker, and Starbucks didn't hit the spot for you, but what about soda? Maybe you are a Coca-Cola fan. Coca-Cola was the world's largest beverage company in 2025, with over 500 soft drink brands sold in more than 200 countries, meaning it generates a lot of data across its value chain. It has data for sourcing, production, distribution, sales, and customer feedback.[2] That is a lot of data that the company can dig into to improve its operations. Coca-Cola has invested in data and AI to help it understand trends, flavor, price, packaging, and customers' preference for healthier options.

Data Use Case 3: American Express

This third real-world example comes from a company I worked for for many years in the past. The American Express Global Business Company (Amex GBT) wanted to improve their online travel program capabilities. They achieved this by investing in smart analytics for their booking software.[3] Essentially, American Express was able to break down its travel ROI into three categories: cost, time, and value. Then, within these categories, KPIs were set to measure and evaluate the performance of the travel plan. Having metrics provided them with visibility.

AI Use Cases

AI Use Case 1: Fraud Detection

In the finance world, we all want our finances and our data protected. It is easy to fall victim to bad actors. For example, in 2024, an employee at a firm in Hong Kong wired $25 million to fraudsters after a deep-faked video call with what appeared to be the company's CFO.[4]

AI has advanced financial planning and wealth management capabilities. Now you can have a robo-advisor that helps a range of clients, including both novice and experienced investors. The AI uses advanced algorithms for activities such as providing personalized investment recommendations and assessing client risk tolerance.[5] Also, machine learning algorithms can spot suspicious transactions in real time which can alert banks and keep our accounts safe and secure.

AI Use Case 2: Manufacturing

AI may not be the technology that physically builds something but it can absolutely still impact the space, especially because the manufacturing space analyzes large amounts of data from sensors and equipment. It can help manage risk and assist predictive maintenance, optimization, strategy, and even robotics.[6]

AI Use Case 3: Agriculture

Okay, did you have agriculture on your bingo card for something data and AI are helping? The potential of data and AI in this industry is huge, such as eliminating hunger and food scarcity. Autonomous tractors and machinery can help by plowing, seeding, and spraying for increased precision and efficiency.[7]

AI can also enable farmers to make smarter data driven decisions. One significant benefit of AI use in agriculture is reducing water wastage. I live in the state of Utah, which is a desert, so I am familiar with the challenges that lack of water can bring. Using data and AI to monitor the moisture in the soil and understand water usage to improve soil, crop use, and drought could be transformative.[8]

Overall, use cases can take the guesswork out of using data and AI. When you see how other companies and industries are implementing these practices, it can help to boost and build one's confidence in data and AI use. So, how can one select a use case that can be implemented? How can you ensure your use case selection is a good one?

Well, let's get one thing out of the way: do not think a use case has to be perfect. In fact, I wonder if any of the data or AI use cases I shared above were first-time use cases. It was likely that those companies did some exploration. We need to remember that we can pivot and iterate on our use cases. We are building confidence in our abilities to use data and AI. If we are expecting a wonderful use case right at the start, we may be setting ourselves up for frustration. So, instead of worrying about it being a perfect use case, plan use cases and test them. Whether the outcome is positive or negative, document them, taking notes on what works and doesn't work. Then, hopefully, we don't repeat the thing that wasn't the best over again.

Let's jump into our checklist for selecting a use case first.

Data and AI Use Case Selection

The Four Rights of Data and AI

Remember the four rights of data and AI? When we are thinking of how to build out a use case and before we go through your use case selection checklist, let's tie the four rights of data and AI to the selection of use cases. Remember, a use case is utilizing data and AI to accomplish a specific goal. Data and AI can inspire so many use cases, so we want to break these four rights of data and AI down to ensure we are successful with our use case work.

The right data and AI is our first "right." This is an important piece of the puzzle. Do we even have access to the right data and AI for the use case we want to accomplish? If we do not have the right data and AI, then can we even accomplish the desired use case? Ensure you study the feasibility of the use case by understanding if you have the data and AI or not.

The second right of data and AI is having the data and AI **at the right time**. We cannot proceed to this if the first right isn't accomplished. Instead, we need to understand the availability of the data and AI at the right time. If the data is there but it is too old or not available for the use cases, then we can kick the use case to the curb.

The third right is having data and AI **that meets our objective**. So, we have selected a use case, and we can see our objective, but if the data and AI don't line up to the use case objective, kick it to the curb. Now, this could be considered the same as the first right: do we have the right data and AI for the right objective? If you want to put this first on your list, that is fine, go for it. But ensure you can accomplish what you need to accomplish. Your objectives should align to the right objectives and goals of the organization.

Finally, do you have **the right data and AI literacy** to accomplish the use case? You may have the first three rights, but run into a wall if you don't have the skills needed to help achieve the use case. So, if you don't have the skills to accomplish what you are looking to do, a new objective you can set for yourself is to develop those skills. Now, another question to ask is: does everyone working on the use case have to have the skills necessary to accomplish it? Not necessarily. You can network and work with others on accomplishing the use case. Don't hesitate to say "I don't have this skill, but this person does," and work with that person to help out.

Overall, as you design a use case, make sure the four rights of data and AI are examined to help you understand if things are feasible or if it is a use case that helps the organization achieve its goals and objectives. Let's look at your checklist for use case selection.

Your Use Case Selection Checklist

As with the other checklists and plans that have been outlined in this book, please don't think this has to be a prescriptive thing for you. To develop your personal confidence with data and AI, ensure you are taking notes from this book and making the things that excite you your own. Modify, iterate, change, and build your data and AI confidence for yourself. What works for one may not work for another and that is okay. It isn't a one-size fits-all, but there is a seat at the data and AI table for everyone.

Here are the steps for selecting a personal or business use case for data and AI use.

CHECK BOX 1: CREATE THE ENVIRONMENT FOR SUCCESS

The first thing we want to do is ensure you have an environment that will empower you with success. If you are looking to use data and AI more, do you have the environment at work (and at home) that will allow you to experiment and learn? At work, do you have leaders who buy in and want the organization to use data and AI more effectively for decisions? Is your organization one that believes in employee development and wants to grow its workforce's skills? Do you have the right resources, such as software or learning material available?

Without these, you may run into difficulties in data and AI work. You want to ensure the environment you work in is prepared for you to take on this work.

CHECK BOX 2: APPROVE YOUR INVESTMENT

What do I mean by approving your investment? Well, it takes time to gain confidence in something, it doesn't just happen overnight. You have to invest, often with time and sometimes with money. In the case of data and AI, ensure you are prepared to invest where appropriate. You will have to invest time in the learning that can take you to the next level with exploring and testing data and AI. You will also want to ensure you have the investment funding to help you succeed. If you want to travel to a country and don't buy the tickets or book the hotel, and just sit around, is the vacation going to happen? No. Same with data and AI work. You will want to drive investment to actually make things work out.

At your organization, if you want to explore and get more confident with data and AI, find out if it is already effectively being used or deployed. If not, then see if you can lead the charge. This may seem intimidating, but you take the lead. With that, though, organizations may not have those who are taking ownership of use cases, and it is an opportunity for you to invest your time and energy to help it happen at your organization. If you don't know how to lead something like this, ask AI because it will help you to realize what skills you may need. Ask AI how to get real buy-in and investment not just from leaders in the organization, but from those you are going to help. This is a project you can take on to really thrive when you are early in your career.

Overall, put the responsibility of becoming more data and AI confident on your own shoulders. Instead, remember it is a journey to develop your confidence over time to get better and better.

CHECK BOX 3: DECIDE YOUR OBJECTIVE

Here we can tie in with Chapter 5 about how to determine where to use data and AI. This plays a part in the four rights of data and AI. Having a solid foundation and objective is a good way to get proof of value from your use case. Notice I didn't say proof of concept. Proof of concept doesn't necessarily mean the end results have value. Instead seek out value from your use case.

Is there a problem, pain, or need that could have a data and/or AI solution? Now, from a business setting, the use case may be easy to find. Does your organization have goals and objectives? Does your team have targets you need to hit? From here, you can find an objective and then get to work and see if there is a way that data and AI can help with the goal or targets. Guess what: even if you don't know if data and/or AI could help, you can prompt AI and ask if there is a way for data and/or AI to help with a certain problem, objective, or goal.

CHECK BOX 4: DETERMINE FEASIBILITY

This is a big one. You can have a great idea come to you for your data and AI confidence boosting, but what do you think might happen if you start the use case and find out it won't work? It may have an adverse effect on your data and AI confidence. So, instead of marching down the road too far with your use case and getting deep into the work, before you start, take the time to understand the feasibility of the work you want to take on.

First, when you have an objective, determine if the data is even accessible, looking at the four rights of data and AI. If you don't have the data, how can you make a data driven decision and build confidence? If the data isn't available, you may be able to create a new use case. It may be to source and gather the right data, to create a strong systematic method to gather that data on an ongoing basis. Just because the data may not be available today doesn't mean we should forget about use cases. Your use case may be a strong one, but then we need to build out the data so that we can perform what needs to be done.

Now, if the data is there, you need to ensure the data is of good quality. To use the data and AI effectively to gain smart decisions, outcomes, and value, we need to have data quality in place. How can you ensure the data is of good quality? Put in a little work to test the data, to review it, to look at it and find if it is good or not. Without the right fuel being put into a car, it may not operate the way it should. The same can be said with data and AI. If we aren't feeding inputs into the use case the way we need it, i.e., high quality data, we may get results that appear to be good but in reality aren't what we need. Do a little work up-front to make the output stronger.

Another important aspect of feasibility is to ensure that the time needed for the work you want to do with data and AI is reasonable. If you have a big idea and then find out it may take you 6–12 months, but you don't have that kind of time to dedicate, that is okay. Instead of trying the big project all at once, divide it into smaller, bite-size pieces. There is no need to overwhelm or stress yourself to build your data and AI confidence. We don't want to build confidence at the detriment of our health and mental wellbeing.

CHECK BOX 5: GET STAKEHOLDERS INVOLVED

Within data and AI work, we want to make sure we are getting stakeholders and the project audience involved. Sometimes, they have the funds we need, so we need to ensure we have their buy-in fully and they are willing participants in the work we are doing. We don't want to do a lot of work on a project without involving them, then show them our new work and progress and they turn it down. We also don't want to get into a project quite a bit and then have them not willing to fund it.

True buy-in is necessary to get data and AI use cases to work and move along. What do I mean by "true buy-in?" I mean they aren't just talking the talk and sounding like they are excited about the project. True buy-in means they are investing in the work and moving forward with it.

When it comes to projects, they can be much more successful when all parties are engaged. This isn't just those who are performing the work, but having their leaders, the groups who benefit from the project, and senior leaders all back the project. Ensure you are working with people in your organization who are going to need to be a part of the project or who already work with data and AI. Network with them, get to know their needs and what they are doing, and, if you can, get them involved in the work. Getting their ideas and insights will empower you to have greater success with project work.

CHECK BOX 6: USE THE THREE CS

The three Cs (curiosity, creativity, and critical thinking) are a powerful way to develop an individual's data and AI confidence.

Curiosity is a wonderful piece of the puzzle to help with data and AI work. Curiosity allows you to dig into something deeper and to drive a more successful use case. When we think of a data and AI use case, one thing we need to ensure we are doing is asking many questions. We need to know why we want to do this use case, who it may impact, what the process will be, and what technology will be involved.

Creativity is something we can harness and bring to data and AI use cases. For a lot of people, data and AI may be mysterious or intimidating, so bringing the human touch of creativity may help a project to succeed more, by thinking differently and innovating. Critical thinking will be very helpful for the use case we are trying to deploy. What impact will it have? Have we allowed bias to creep into the use case? What could go wrong? Does it make sense? Allow your critical thinking muscles to be used and don't become too reliant on the data and AI or assume they are correct; bring the human element to the table.

Overall, the three Cs should be integral to your data and AI work and use cases. Utilize them on an ongoing basis and ask lots of questions. Ensure the work is moving forward to solve a real-world problem or use case. If you find that the answers to the questions aren't what you want, that is okay; shift and move forward with a new use case.

CHECK BOX 7: HAVE FUN

Allow data and AI to be things that you do for fun. You don't have to be an AI specialist or data scientist to enjoy working with data and AI. Bring them into projects you are already working on. Move them forward with projects, goals, and things that have value. Focus on the good things you enjoy and get to work.

Your Data and AI Deployment Checklist

Now that you have your use case and are moving forward with it, then success is automatically going to come, right? If it involves stakeholders and others, they will just adopt whatever you are doing, right? Well, of course the answer is no.

The reality is, with data and AI, we may be moving things in a direction that brings changes to well-established processes. That is a hard reality for people sometimes. Change and innovation can be wonderful things, but many people may not enjoy them. That is okay. With data and AI, when people can see the value derived from the work that has been done and they are shown how to adopt and use it correctly, it may then be easier to drive its widespread adoption. Let's take a look at some steps you can take in your data and AI deployment.

Step 1: Create a Compelling Vision and Narrative

To get people to buy into what you are doing, a compelling vision and story will be key to getting people involved in doing the use case.

It may be the difference between people being able to change and not being willing to change. Let's make sure we understand that data points don't change people, narratives do. So, for your work within data and AI deployment, ensure the story and narrative you are sharing is helping the audience understand the data and AI work that has taken place, that has driven a decision, and how you are going to deploy it.

One thing you may not be comfortable with is creating a narrative to help people get on board. Let's help you build some confidence. From Literacy Ideas, we learn the following steps, that I have adapted for a data and AI context:[9]

1 **Set the scene.** With data and AI, set the scene of whatever the use case is and the benefits that can be gained from implementing it.
2 **Cast the characters.** Who are the stakeholders in the use case? Who do you need to have involved to make the deployment succeed?
3 **Determine the problem.** What is your use case going to solve? If you created something cool but you don't know what issue it solved, get back to the drawing board. People are busy and if you bring something to them and they don't know what is expected of them, they are unlikely to get on board.
4 **The narrative peak.** What is the big point of the data and AI story you are sharing? Is it an insight that can help your clients? A new product idea?
5 **The resolution.** Finally, what are the next steps for your data and AI project? Ensure your narrative is one that can be clearly implemented and one that people get on board with.

Step 2: Create Your Deployment Strategy

Yes, you need to figure out the strategy for deploying your data and/or AI use case. This can be a simple strategy, or it may be complicated, depending on the use case. Do you like getting an email saying you have mandatory training to take? If you don't, do you think others want to get an email saying they now have to deploy something? Instead, think about strategies you will take to overcome this resistance.

Within your strategy, ensure you have created a roadmap for the deployment. How long will the deployment take and what are the key milestones along the way? If people are busy and we are now trying to give them work to do with data and AI, adding to their plate could hinder the roadmap. So, instead, get involved with the stakeholders to get a good grasp of the timeline that will help your plan succeed. Understand if there will be financial investments or not. Ensure you are creating a reasonable roadmap with milestones that are achievable. If you are building milestones that aren't realistic, you may lose your audience quickly when the use case is deployed. Instead, make milestones measurable and reasonable. Ensure you are moving forward in a strategic manner.

It is like the training and running of an ultra-marathon. You can create a roadmap and strategy to prepare you for a large race, but find you need to adjust as you go. Maybe you get injured. Maybe weather impacts you. For whatever reason, you have to be flexible. Then, you "deploy" the race (run it). This is similar to how you should be thinking about your data and AI deployment strategy. You do the work, you are flexible with it, and then you march forward to help you succeed.

Step 3: Communication Plan

As part of your deployment strategy, craft a strong communication plan. From Project Manager, we learn some things about building the communication plan:[10]

- **Put communication objectives in place.** Laying out what the communication plan should achieve is crucial. Maybe it is just to give information, maybe it is to persuade, maybe it is to illustrate the "why" of the data and AI strategy.
- **Pinpoint stakeholder communication needs.** Building the communication for your intended audience is important, as they may have different needs. Some of these requirements can include the following:
    - Frequency: How often do they like to be contacted? We don't want to bore them or annoy them with too much communication. Some may like more and others may prefer less. So, ensure

  you understand the audience and how often they would like communication.
  - Channel: We have that in the next section, but ensure you are communicating in the right channel, i.e., by phone, or by email.
  - Style: What do they like? Do they like long paragraphs with all the details, or do they like short bullet points? Design the communication style to the style of the audience. Sometimes, this means you have different styles for the same communication. That is okay. Get to know your audience and style according to them. Ultimately, ensure that the communications convey the use case clearly and concisely.
- **Set communication delivery channels.** As mentioned above, the appropriate channel should be utilized to broadcast the communication. Do you have people who still like to receive a phone call? Do people want a live webinar or recorded video? Do you have people who like email or Slack or Teams? When you know your audience, you can know what the right communication delivery channel is. Don't just assume it to be this or that, as some people may not respond.
- **Establish metrics.** As part of your communication with the stakeholders, you can establish the metrics you want to monitor the use case. You can set frequency of monitoring to their preference. This will play a part for us in the monitoring and iteration section below.
- **Create a communication schedule.** It can be a delicate balance to create a schedule that is not too frequent or too infrequent. If it is too frequent, we may annoy people. If too much time passes by, enthusiasm can wane away.

Step 4: Provide Appropriate Training

Okay, if we are deploying a data and/or AI use case and the users don't have the skills to utilize the use case effectively, what will happen? It may become an expensive miss, and we don't want that. Instead, ensure you are providing the right training for the new data and/or AI use case. It may require some technical skills; it may require some literacy, but ensure there is proper training for the audience who will be using the new use case.

The importance of training cannot be overstated. When it comes to developing skills and confidence in data and AI, we need to tailor it to the person. We can design training around using an assessment to find where an individual's gaps are. Then, we build the training out. This can involve investment from a company or individual, or you can find some free courses.

When the majority of people don't go to school for a degree in data and AI, training becomes something important for professionals and individuals to take on. We want to ensure we are helping provide the right training at the right time for the right objective. We don't want to bombard people, as they may have a busy job. We want to help them be empowered with confidence and skills.

Step 5: Monitor, Feedback Loop, and Iterate

The last step in deployment is to ensure, as part of the strategy, you create a way to monitor the deployment to see whether you are getting the success you had hoped you would. What metrics did you choose to monitor the deployment? Then remember the cadence (once a month, quarterly, etc.) you chose for communication. Use it to ensure these metrics are being communicated.

Also, allow feedback to come to you from the users during your monitoring. The reality is, if we aren't getting feedback from the parties utilizing the new use case, we may be missing out on vital information to make it the best we can. So, ensure you have a feedback channel to get information from your users.

Finally, with the monitoring and feedback, you are then able to iterate and improve upon the use case. Take the time to assess the data coming in on your use case. Take the time to see what adjustments and iterations you can make. Then, do it. Actually implement feedback and push ahead with improvements in your use case.

Keeping Momentum Going

Now, when it comes to having a use case that provides value and achieves success, one thing we want to maintain is momentum for an organization. We don't want to gain joy, success, growth, and then have it fade away over time. So, what can you do to maintain momentum and have it continue? Here are some strategies.

Celebrate the Wins

As use cases succeed, celebrate the wins. I don't mean you need to spend a lot of time every time something succeeds. Instead, use moments to recognize team members, and share the results and what went well. Celebrating small moments can have a large impact on the organization.

Monthly Webinars or Office Hours

As you continue to progress with data and AI work, have monthly lunch and learns, webinars, or open office hours, where people can hear about the success, hear what is working well, and discuss new topics. They could be opportunities to learn, grow, to increase skills. It could be an opportunity to have a senior leader who believes in the work talk about why the organization should too.

Newsletter

Create a newsletter for people to read, nothing long, but it can share the wins that have happened, the latest trends in data and AI, and learning opportunities. Don't make this a long newsletter, page after page. Don't even make the articles or discussions of topics long. Instead, provide links so that if people are interested in learning more, they can be guided to the longer discussion. You could even have a book recommendation corner, which provides opportunities for people to find ones that are on topics that may interest them.

Community

Create a data and AI community in the organization where people can converse about and chat about successes and what is working, ask questions, and grow together. Enable the community and empower it, don't let it shrink away.

Conclusion

Through this chapter we have looked into the value of use cases. Remember that not all use cases are big. To help you develop your data and AI confidence, a small personal use case could be beneficial. You may find from this that something worked the way you intended it. That is great. Then, you can get to work on expanding your use case.

Remember, in a use case, the stakeholders and audience matter greatly. If you are building out a use case in your business, you don't want to get running on it, only to find out that the audience doesn't like what you have built and pushes back heavily. Deploying these use cases can be difficult, as stakeholders can find change hard to accept. Therefore, getting the stakeholders involved is key to success.

Finally, remember the importance of communication throughout a use case and its deployment. Ensure you are communicating openly and transparently. Don't hide information away from people, good or bad. If bad things arise, such as the data painting a picture that isn't going in the direction we want or need, it is better to voice it and create a solution to overcome the negative.

You have a seat at this table. After finishing this chapter, take a minute to think about and write down potential use cases you can build and deploy.

KEY TAKEAWAYS

- Utilize use cases to help drive your data and AI work.
- Work toward value from the use cases.
- You can utilize the use case checklist from this chapter, but make it your own.

Notes

1 Systems+. 8 Case Studies and Real World Examples of How Big Data Has Helped Keep on Top of Competition, February 15, 2022, systems-plus.com/8-case-studies-and-real-world-examples-of-how-big-data-has-helped-keep-on-top-of-competition/ (archived at https://perma.cc/6WN4-4M8V)

2 Systems+. 8 Case Studies and Real World Examples of How Big Data Has Helped Keep on Top of Competition, February 15, 2022, systems-plus.com/8-case-studies-and-real-world-examples-of-how-big-data-has-helped-keep-on-top-of-competition/ (archived at https://perma.cc/6WN4-4M8V)

3 Systems+. 8 Case Studies and Real World Examples of How Big Data Has Helped Keep on Top of Competition, February 15, 2022, systems-plus.com/8-case-studies-and-real-world-examples-of-how-big-data-has-helped-keep-on-top-of-competition/ (archived at https://perma.cc/6WN4-4M8V)

4 M. Novikova. Four Approaches to Using Machine Learning in Real-Time Fraud Detection (with Real-World Examples), Xenoss, July 3, 2025, xenoss.io/blog/real-time-ai-fraud-detection-in-banking (archived at https://perma.cc/A284-DTBP)

5 B. Marr. 15 Amazing Real-World Applications of AI Everyone Should Know About, *Forbes*, May 10, 2023, www.forbes.com/sites/bernardmarr/2023/05/10/15-amazing-real-world-applications-of-ai-everyone-should-know-about/ (archived at https://perma.cc/97TV-45AW)

6 B. Marr. 15 Amazing Real-World Applications of AI Everyone Should Know About, *Forbes*, May 10, 2023, www.forbes.com/sites/bernardmarr/2023/05/10/15-amazing-real-world-applications-of-ai-everyone-should-know-about/ (archived at https://perma.cc/97TV-45AW)

7 B. Marr. 15 Amazing Real-World Applications of AI Everyone Should Know About, *Forbes*, May 10, 2023, www.forbes.com/sites/bernardmarr/2023/05/10/15-amazing-real-world-applications-of-ai-everyone-should-know-about/ (archived at https://perma.cc/97TV-45AW)

8 A. Barinov. How AI for Agriculture Is Transforming Farming: 10 Real-World Use Cases, intelliarts, July 10, 2025, intelliarts.com/blog/ai-in-agriculture-use-cases/ (archived at https://perma.cc/7BW2-LWED)

9 K. Cummins. Narrative Writing: A Complete Guide for Teachers and Students, Literacy Ideas for Teachers and Students, December 9, 2024, literacyideas.com/narrative-writing/ (archived at https://perma.cc/2HTR-H5QR)

10 B. Schwartz. How to Make a Change Management Communication Plan, ProjectManager, July 9, 2024, www.projectmanager.com/blog/change-management-communication (archived at https://perma.cc/76JZ-33GS)

PART TWO

The Human Factor

7

Why Human and Emotional Intelligence Still Matter in the Age of Data and AI

Let me ask you a question: as you watch movies like *iRobot* or *Ex-Machina* or even *The Terminator* (although I am not sure if time travel is anywhere near on the horizon), how does it make you feel to see AI ruling over the planet? Does it make sense to you or make you feel good about what you are seeing? Does it give you a good feeling inside to turn over these things to something that may not have emotion or compassion?

We are human and like the human touch. Although AI may be powerful, it still, at the time of writing, does not understand the human experience the way we do. It does not capture compassion or empathy when needed. It can appear to, but may actually be cold and process-oriented. This can get in the way of data and AI success because humans want warmth, compassion, and to feel like they are understood. The other side is that we as humans have knowledge that can apply to decisions, we have emotions and intelligence that should be combined with and not superseded by the data and AI.

Now, when we think of data and AI, we may think that human skills will be less valued and therefore humans will be left behind. Does gut feel and intuition play a part in Engineered Intelligence? Remember our formula:

Data + AI + IQ + EQ = Engineered Intelligence

Our formula has the data and AI side, which matter. This is the technical side which provides knowledge and intelligence in ways that we are not as good at doing. The other side has the human elements of IQ and EQ, which are equally as important.

I want us to start to think of humans being energized and empowered in the age of data and AI. We humans are being supercharged toward success. Think about your ability to be creative, to take ideas to new stages and areas; think about your ability to ask questions and critically assess. We, as humans, should not be replaced but enhanced and augmented by AI. Allow AI to be your partner, at your side to help you with these areas.

Now, there may be some tasks that are automated and taken from us, but can't we use that new free time to be more strategic, innovative, and empowered? Yes. With the tools at our fingertips we are even more productive.

Another thing to think about is there will be new jobs created in the future. Even if jobs are eliminated, this does not mean a net loss in jobs. We may need to look at the future of jobs from a different lens. Not job elimination, but job redefining. That is okay to do. We should look to redefine and do things in a new way as we handle the world of data and AI and its evolution.

I hope this encourages you to view the advancements coming to us positively. You have a seat at the table, your ideas and gut feel matter, your creativity and questions are good. Bring them to life. By developing your data and AI confidence, you are finding where you sit at the table of data and AI.

In this chapter, we will cover the following:

- Thinking about what it means to be human.
- Defining both human intelligence (HI) measured in IQ (intelligence quotient), and emotional intelligence (EI) measured in EQ (emotional quotient).
- Why HI and EI matter in the world of data and AI.

- How a person can develop their skills and abilities within HI and EI, and why they should.
- Growth vs. a stagnant mindset.

Now, let us jump into what it means to be human.

What Does It Mean to Be Human?

Ask yourself a question: what does it mean to be human? Really think about it for a minute or two. What does it mean to be you? What makes you unique from other humans? What talents, ideas, thoughts do you have? I encourage you to write down things that make you, you. I could write: journaling, writing and reading books, strategic thinking, rugby, and family. As a human, I am pretty passionate, I like to push my limits, and I like to grow.

Uniquely human characteristics are consciousness, emotions, and empathy. Consciousness can be defined as awareness of ourselves and our thoughts and feelings. Now, when we look at AI, does it have consciousness? Does it demonstrate emotions or empathy?

A conversation with the Google Gemini AI tool, asking whether it was conscious, revealed an interesting response. It highlighted that although it can process information and respond in ways that seem intelligent, it acts on algorithms and data it has been trained on and does not have subjective experience or awareness of the world in the same way humans do. However, the way we define consciousness is based on human experience, so other forms of intelligence, whether artificial or biological, could have a different form of awareness.

As mentioned above, both emotion and empathy also signify that humans are unique. Of the 8.7 million species on the earth, we are the only ones that paint self-portraits, have walked on the moon, and worship gods.[1] Why is that? What is it that is a part of us that causes these things to occur? Our advanced intelligence (IQ and EQ) is one of the things that differentiate us from other species and now differentiate us from AI.

Emotion is defined as something we experience that is subjective and prompts a mental, physical, or behavioral reaction.

Empathy, being able to understand other people's feelings or experience, is an area which really distinguishes us as humans because AI can only imitate it. In the world of data and AI, having an empathetic mentor for example can be a good thing as you are developing your confidence.

The reality is, we do not know exactly what the future of AI is going to hold but we can tackle our own future by preparing for it and driving forward with what makes us unique: namely our consciousness, emotions, and empathy. Each one of us is unique. We have stories. We have abilities that maybe others do not have exactly like us. So, by developing our confidence, we can use our human skills to be enabled and empowered by AI—not overtaken by it.

Shared in the World Economic Forum's Future of Jobs Report 2025 was a list of the top ten fastest growing skills by 2030.[2] The list is below:

1. AI and big data
2. networks and cybersecurity
3. technological literacy
4. creative thinking
5. resilience, flexibility, and agility
6. curiosity and lifelong learning
7. leadership and social influence
8. talent management
9. analytical thinking
10. environmental stewardship

One thing that stands out to me in the fastest growing skills by 2030 is that the majority of them are human related, showing that human skills are still essential for success. Therefore, take confidence from the fact that success is not purely reliant on data and AI skills. This is great as we know where to focus our efforts to thrive, grow, develop, and look to enhance our technical skills for success.

TIP

Consider the three Cs of data literacy again: curiosity, creativity, and critical thinking. Looking at this list, skill numbers 4, 6, and 9 align closely with them.

Does this excite you? Does it help you to feel less nervous about AI? Take the time to look at yourself and have an honest assessment of where your skills are today. If you have gaps, then attack them and grow.

One exercise you can do is prompt AI to do a self-assessment about the human skills that exist in this list. Then, you can take the new assessment, see where your gaps are, and define a way to empower and improve yourself. Here is an example of doing this:

> "I am looking to enhance my skills in the following key areas:
>
> - technological literacy
> - creative thinking
> - resilience, flexibility, and agility
> - curiosity and lifelong learning
> - leadership and social influence
> - analytical thinking
> - environmental stewardship
>
> Please create an assessment that can empower me to grow in my knowledge and work toward a better future for myself in my career. Can you please provide the answer key, scoring, and steps to improve in the areas where I am weak? Thank you for your help."

Remember, the prompt response is going to be better for you depending on the clarity of the prompt. I could have shared more details about what my current abilities were in these skills, and I could have shared career goals and plans. You can make it more about yourself. Maybe you test this prompt multiple times until you arrive at an assessment you feel fits you. That is great. Ensure you are building this not according to me, but according to you, your goals, your visions, and your dreams.

The assessment Gemini provided gave me a score scale of 1 to 5, where 1 represented "strongly disagree" and five "strongly agree." Then, the AI broke questions down for the categories of technological literacy; creative thinking; resilience, flexibility, and agility; curiosity and lifelong learning; leadership and social influence; and, finally, environmental stewardship. You therefore have the ability to rank yourself against each of the questions by the scoring system and look at the results the AI gave. You can further prompt the AI to provide recommended resources that focus on the listed areas. Remember to detail the types of resources that you like, whether that be articles, books, online videos, or podcasts.

One thing you can try is input your assessment answers back into the AI and ask it what you can do to improve. Play around and experiment here. By experimenting and developing, you may find that you are able to learn and develop even more confidence and skills because you are not just taking things at face value.

Intelligence Quotient and Emotional Quotient

You have probably heard the term "IQ" before. You may think IQ can have a big impact on AI, and you would not be wrong. Our knowledge and ideas can play a part with AI. Technically speaking, intelligence quotient is a number that indicates how developed your cognitive abilities are.[3] Essentially, IQ is your intelligence; let's look at it as your "book smarts" or "academic smarts." IQ is a powerful thing that can empower human beings in their careers, but it isn't the be all and end all of intelligence. We will discuss the other type of intelligence, emotional intelligence, in just a bit.

Let us take a look at some well-known people and their IQ scores:[4]

- Stephen Hawking: 160
- Albert Einstein: 160–190
- Christopher Michael Langan: 190–210
- Kim Ung-Yong: 210
- K. Visalini: 225

- Christopher Hirata: 225
- Marilyn Vos Savant: 228
- Terence Tao: 225–230

A score within the range of 85–115 would be considered average and at approximately the same level as 68 percent of the population. A score of about 115 is considered gifted. Above 145 is associated with genius.[5] However, as mentioned above, IQ is just one part of our equation:

Data + AI + IQ + EQ = Engineered Intelligence

Emotional quotient (emotional intelligence) can be defined as "the ability to perceive, understand, and manage one's own emotions and relationships. It involves being aware of emotions in oneself and others and using this awareness to guide thinking and behavior."[6] For example, when you think of AI and what it is doing in the world today, what feelings pop up? Do you recognize the feeling; is it anxiety, stress, excitement? Now, think about your ability to read others' emotions. Can you have empathy for the other person?

In a business setting, it can matter greatly to understand your own emotions and manage them. If we were to only react with our instinctive first thoughts, this may not be the right thing to do. We need to be controlled, aware, and then we can act. With a good awareness and knowledge of ours and others' emotions, we guide our behavior and thinking.

Emotional intelligence is something I feel may be more important than IQ. We can be book smart but not understand people, which in turn causes frustration and issues. Instead of deploying and utilizing data and AI in a way that our audience may be comfortable with, we perhaps don't understand our teams well enough. Maybe the team is apprehensive of AI as they think it will replace them, so they don't use it. Remember, our formula is Data + AI + IQ + EQ = Engineered Intelligence, so we don't want to leave out a part of the formula.

Some examples of how emotional intelligence helps when deploying data and AI solutions are detailed below.

Example 1: Driving a Marketing Campaign

When we think of increasing confidence in our abilities to use data and AI, understanding how the four pieces of the formula work together can help you. Imagine you are helping with a new marketing campaign at your business. For this new campaign, you start off by analyzing what data you have. You look into it to understand the quality, the access that you have to the data or if you need to request access to the data, and that you have multiple data points that will help. Now, let me clarify the access part here. Some data may be restricted within companies and so not everyone has access to it. So, when analyzing data, you may be required to request access to some of it so you can perform your work.

Next, you dive into the artificial intelligence tools that are at your fingertips. You find that there is some information you can gather through a large language model, and you want to help harness the power of predictive modeling to show what could happen. Your organization has a data team that helps drive some machine learning. You want to use it for the deployment of knowledge for the marketing campaign.

Thirdly, you dive into you and your team's human intelligence. You know that you are pretty good at analyzing the data as it comes through, but you aren't advanced in your data skills. On the other hand, you have a team member, let's call them Tim. Tim is good at analysis and great at getting information out of advanced analytics. There is a problem, though.

In the fourth step, using our emotional intelligence, you know that Tim is a bit frustrated because he is getting messages from multiple people for requests, some that are outside of your team. He does not appreciate all the requests at this time and you are aware of this, so you utilize your emotional intelligence skills to determine how to approach him and get him on board with the project. For example, you could acknowledge how busy he is and politely ask when he thinks he will have time to do these advanced analytics.

As you can see, it isn't just about having IQ, data, and AI. You need EQ to get Tim onboard to help you with the project.

Example 2: Job Reductions

One area of business that is difficult to navigate is when job numbers are reduced. I have been a part of organizations that have done layoffs before, and they aren't easy. Let's imagine your organization is looking to put more work into AI, one piece of our formula, which reduces the need for a few jobs. You may be in your role and fear being let go. You wonder if being early in your career is going to count against you. This can cause you to feel anxiety and negative emotions. With this, as announcements are made, you are given data and information that show why reductions are done. You have the IQ on how to use the data, and it helps you to understand the "why" behind things. But to harness success here, emotional intelligence is key, as you need to be able to help those affected, help culture succeed, and help yourself in a difficult situation.

With this in mind, you need to ensure you have good, smart conversations with those being displaced. Then, after the organizational move is in place, you need emotional intelligence to help those remaining. This also means you don't try to push things too fast. You need to allow those in the company to express their feelings.

When it comes to data and AI confidence, having a good ability to use data and AI with your human intelligence is key. But emotional intelligence for both you and those you work with may be more important in some situations.

Why IQ and EQ Matter in the World of Data and AI

Now, the question you may be asking is how IQ and EQ play a part in data and AI. Well, AI is continuously evolving, and some people may be uncomfortable with this. This response is okay, because what matters is what you do with your thoughts, and reading this book about data and AI skills and developing more confidence is a great step. As the AI moves, and it may be rapid, your ideas and knowledge can be applied with the advancements of AI. Developing knowledge around the latest trends with AI is key. Developing confidence and dealing with excitement or fear appropriately can help you with the continued evolution of data and AI too.

In the world of data, making smart, data driven decisions, combining both human intelligence and technology, matters. IQ can be seen as our own personal data points, which can be added to or used to evaluate the technical data. For example, the world of data has different roles and positions, from data architects and engineers to analytics and scientists, some of which are highly technical. The technical aspect may be coding the architecture on the back end of the data work, or the front-end statistical analysis that will help bring data to life with insight and information. By having IQ on how to do these things, understanding the ins and outs, you are combining IQ with the technology architecture to derive value.

EQ also matters with data driven decisions. From the book *How Minds Change* I learned that data doesn't change minds; narrative does.[7] We as humans like stories. Narrative plays a part in how we perceive things, how we relate to them. When we want to use data to make smarter decisions, we need to create narrative. Here, we can bring in our EQ to move forward, helping people get on board, relate to, and bring success to the data driven decision we want to have happen.

What about AI with IQ and EQ? AI absolutely matters with IQ. Think back to our assessment prompt earlier in this chapter. How many of us have a background of crafting assessments and implementing them at organizations? That may not be many of us, and that is okay. Herein we can combine AI with our personal IQ and EQ. We can input the prompt, giving it ideas about who we are or what the organization does. Then, we can ask the AI for help and drive forward a solution to utilize, using our IQ to consider how we can model the data correctly, visualize it, and apply it to business decisions. Then, EQ can come into play because we need to bring decisions to life, taking the prompt response and knowing how to utilize it within a team. EQ is also key when dealing with anxiety about what AI can do.

Here, we can bring empathy to the table. If we are in an organization where we are being told that AI is here to stay and we just need to get over our nerves and anxiety, that isn't necessarily the right message for us to hear. Instead, we can use our EQ and self-awareness to understand how this will impact us and our co-workers, and even if we don't have a leadership role, we can lead by example in using AI, developing the skills for it. We can also help our co-workers to innovate and be empowered themselves. Instead of being full of fear and anxiety, if we get to know people and understand how they operate, what will help them to adopt and adapt well, and what will help them be resilient, then we set ourselves up better for success.

Overall, intelligence and emotional quotient can help you move forward with data and AI. We need to grow in these areas in our lives, but how can we do that? The following section will outline some ways we can develop these skills.

Developing and Improving Our IQ and EQ

Ask yourself a question: do you think you can personally develop your IQ and EQ? If you don't, well, our next section will talk about growth mindset versus stagnant mindset. But I want you to believe today that you can develop your IQ and EQ, so let's give you a few ways to do it.

Studying and Reading

I love to study and read. Maybe you don't, but you at least have this book to start your journey. The reality is, to help drive our IQ, we can study topics, take notes, and learn. Knowledge is power. The more we know, we can help to drive more solutions, prompt AI better, or understand how to better tell a story to help persuade or change minds. Find ways to learn that you enjoy. If you don't like reading, maybe you use audio books. Maybe you like podcasts. Maybe you are a visual learner, so you watch videos to help you advance. One key thing to think about is how you will apply studying and reading.

To help this learning stick and become a part of your knowledge base, take notes, write down what you are learning, and experiment. Without writing and applying the knowledge in some way, we may not remember it as well. So, do what you can to remember what you study. One thing you can do, and hopefully this makes sense, is put the learning you are gaining into a song. Do you find that you can remember the words to a song you haven't heard in a long time? Well, think about adding data and AI notes to a song and see if that helps it to stick in your head.

If you are early in your career, find how the studying and reading can be applied to the work you are doing, the skills you want to develop in your career, and the career track you want to follow. By applying the principles to your work and career, it may propel you forward.

Practice Makes Permanent

Don't use the phrase "practice makes perfect," because perfection is unattainable: we simply want to experiment with data and AI to help you develop confidence and ability. Plus, what if you practice things imperfectly, so then your habits still remain imperfect?

You may ask: how do I practice EQ? Well, you dig in and you talk to people, you listen to what is going on with them, and you put yourself in their shoes. The reality that is people do fear AI and may be intimidated by data. Try to understand how they are feeling. You may have a wonderful solution that you are thinking of implementing, but if your EQ isn't high, they won't get onboard.

Practice the Art of Listening

Have you ever had a friend, partner, someone you could trust and talk to about things going on in your life? Have you ever spoken to someone who just listens well and then they offer up good solutions to help you with whatever you were talking about? Listening improves both our IQ and EQ; if we get good at listening, we can learn more. As the Dalai Lama said, "When you speak, you only repeat what you already know. But if you listen, you can learn new things."[8] If all we do is talk, how can we listen to someone teaching us? How are we learning what's going on with someone and how can we address it well?

Don't just listen to respond. Listen to learn. If we are trying to think of how to respond to what someone is saying instead of taking in what they say, we may miss out.

Ask More Questions

Asking questions is key to growth within IQ and EQ. Ask questions of AI platforms, of mentors, of other experts, to learn new topics. Curiosity, part of the top ten fastest growing skills by 2030, as covered earlier in the chapter, can help spark learning and development. Ask lots of questions and learn more and more. Below are a few more ways to improve your IQ and EQ.

IQ:[9]

- memory training, e.g. jigsaws or crosswords
- executive control tasks, e.g. brainteasers
- visuospatial reasoning activities, e.g. 3D models
- relational training, e.g. amount comparisons
- engaging in continued education

EQ:[10]

- Name your emotions: Without recognizing and naming our own personal emotions, how can we understand and deal with them?
- Be open to direct and constructive feedback: Don't always take just positive feedback, because how are we going to grow in our careers and lives if all we hear is positive? Like breaking a muscle down, we can grow stronger with constructive feedback.
- Understand your responses to other people: Take note of how you respond to people. Is it direct and reactive? Or are you proactive and thoughtful?
- Acknowledge your strengths and vulnerabilities: One thing we don't want to do is continually avoid or deny our vulnerabilities and weaknesses. Work on a mindset that allows you to be honest about where you currently stand.
- Understand how you deal with stress: Write down how you deal with stress. Then, find ways to improve upon areas that may be a weakness.
- Think about how your choices impact others' emotions: Take the time to have empathy and put yourselves in their shoes. Then, use that to be proactive in your actions.

Growth vs. Stagnant Mindset

Those who have a growth mindset "believe their talents can be developed (through hard work, good strategies, and input from others)."[11] Be honest with yourself: do you feel like you can learn data and AI? If you do, then you may have a growth mindset already, but if you don't you may have a stagnant (fixed) mindset.

With a fixed mindset, people believe that their skills are fixed, that they are born with them and you reach them in adulthood. With this mindset, people don't think they can change these skills.[12] So, a person with a fixed mindset may think they cannot learn data and AI. Of these two mindsets, growth mindsets are a lot more likely to succeed with data and AI confidence. How does mindset link to areas of the human in this chapter? Let's take a look and start off with the World Economic Forum skills that highlighted the importance of the three Cs to illustrate mindset here. I will start off with creative thinking.

Do you think of yourself as being creative? Children are very creative, but as we get older we can lose this skill. To say "I am not creative" is to fall into the stagnant mindset. But saying "I can learn to be creative again" represents a growth mindset. The first step to having a growth mindset is knowing that you can improve.

Another piece from the World Economic Forum list is analytical thinking. To be stagnant with a mindset with analytical or critical thinking means that we may say to ourselves "I can't figure this out," or "There is no way I am going to be able to analyze this," or even "This has to be the answer, there isn't anything else to do." Instead, a growth mindset may say "I don't know how to analyze this, but I am going to find out" and then you get to work to learn. The growth mindset is about learning and potential. If you go through things you can't do, then you may have just cemented yourself to not grow. Don't go on that route.

Finally, let's look at curiosity and lifelong learning. In this case, if you are stagnant, you will believe that you aren't able to be a lifelong learner, or you tell yourself you can't learn something. If you have a growth mindset, you may be super curious and think you can learn anything. So, you apply this approach within your role consistently and you are a lifelong learner.

Now, how does a growth mindset tie to IQ and EQ, and how does a stagnant mindset affect our IQ and EQ? It may be clear now, but let's discuss this. With our IQ, our intelligence, if we feel we can't learn more or we feel like there isn't any more to learn, we may have a stagnant mindset. This can hinder our progress and can hinder how much human intelligence we can bring to our data and AI work. So, instead, a growth mindset makes us ready to take in more knowledge and intelligence. We are curious, we are digging in, we are learning and growing. We are lifelong learners. In your career, there will be many people you come across, many you learn from. With a growth mindset, you can take notes, literally if you want, to learn and grow from others. Don't miss out on this chance to grow your intelligence.

If you have a growth mindset with emotional intelligence, EQ, you feel similarly. I may not have the most empathy, but I can learn it. I may not be very self-aware of my skills and what I do, but I can learn it. With a stagnant mindset, we are sitting and thinking we don't have a characteristic and can't learn it. Don't settle, and don't cement yourself as complete. Grow and learn.

Conclusion

The world is moving fast with AI, and if we aren't careful we may be passed over in work and left behind. Data and AI may have technical aspects, but don't forget the human element. Being human matters. Remember the top ten fastest growing skills by 2030, where the majority are human skills. My three Cs of data literacy are curiosity, creativity, and critical thinking. These apply in our lives to how we successfully use data and AI. Don't let your critical thinking muscle grow weak. Don't let your curiosity waste away. Don't forget to work on your creativity. Being empathetic and willing to help yourself and your organizations move forward with data and AI.

Again, you and your personal IQ and EQ have a seat at the data and AI table, it may be that you just need to find your way to that seat and what you get to feast on. Don't stress out about what is going on around you. Manage it, manage your IQ and EQ. Build your confidence and skills, and work toward Engineered Intelligence.

KEY TAKEAWAYS

- We can continue to learn and grow our IQ and EQ with a growth mindset.
- The World Economic Forum's top ten fastest growing skills by 2030 includes six that are human-focused.
- Your IQ and EQ matter with data and AI; do not forget your personal knowledge.

Notes

1 E. Elster. How Are Humans Different from Other Animals? They Have a Uniquely Open-Ended Culture, University of Culture, April 3, 2025, www.universityofcalifornia.edu/news/how-are-humans-different-other-animals-they-have-uniquely-open-ended-culture (archived at https://perma.cc/MU7V-M4LW)

2 World Economic Forum. Future of Jobs Report 2025: 78 Million New Job Opportunities by 2030 but Urgent Upskilling Needed to Prepare Workforces, January 7, 2025. www.weforum.org/press/2025/01/future-of-jobs-report-2025-78-million-new-job-opportunities-by-2030-but-urgent-upskilling-needed-to-prepare-workforces/ (archived at https://perma.cc/G3FS-PJ5Y)

3 A. Patel. What Is IQ: How It's Measured, Is It Important, & More, IQtest.net, December 26, 2023, iqtest.net/blog/what-is-iq (archived at https://perma.cc/4Q5G-N33X)

4 H. Gupta. 12 People Who Have the Highest IQ in the World, ScienceABC, December 17, 2023, www.scienceabc.com/humans/people-who-have-the-highest-iq-in-the-world-html.html (archived at https://perma.cc/SLW6-2LTH)

5 A. Patel. What Is IQ: How It's Measured, Is It Important, & More, IQtest.net, December 26, 2023, iqtest.net/blog/what-is- iq (archived at https://perma.cc/4Q5G-N33X)

6 M. B. Frothingham. Emotional Intelligence (EQ), SimplyPsychology, January 29, 2024, www.simplypsychology.org/emotional-intelligence.html (archived at https://perma.cc/KUW3-FEH4)

7 D. McRaney (2022) *How Minds Change: The Surprising Science of Belief, Opinion, and Persuasion*, Portfolio/Penguin, New York

8 Lukas. The Dalai Lama on Listening, How to Live, how-to-live.de/en/the-dalai-lama-about-listening/ (archived at https://perma.cc/NC2Q-35FQ)

9 E. M. S. Lockett. 8 Ways to Increase Your IQ Levels, Healthline, July 29, 2022, www.healthline.com/health/how-to-increase-iq (archived at https://perma.cc/K3V6-NCEZ)

10 H. Brown. What Is Emotional Intelligence? +23 Ways To Improve It, PositivePsychology.com, November 14, 2018, positivepsychology.com/emotional-intelligence-eq/ (archived at https://perma.cc/C4PQ-CHRP)

11 C. Dweck. What Having a "Growth Mindset" Actually Means, *Harvard Business Review*, January 13, 2016, hbr.org/2016/01/what-having-a-growth-mindset-actually-means (archived at https://perma.cc/H9PQ-7E6G)

12 J. Smith. Growth vs. Fixed Mindset: How What You Think Affects What You Achieve, Mindset Health, September 25, 2020, www.mindsethealth.com/matter/growth-vs-fixed-mindset (archived at https://perma.cc/TS37-9PUF)

8

Applying Your Human and Emotional Intelligence to Data and AI Decisions

Following the previous chapter on IQ (human intelligence) and EQ (emotional intelligence), we can transition into how we can apply these to unemotional data and AI. It is easy to understand that data isn't "emotional." But what about AI?

AI is artificial *intelligence*: if AI has intelligence, considered to be on par with human intelligence, could we just run with whatever the AI says and not worry about anything else, presuming it understands human emotion? Remember AI gains its intelligence from the data it is trained on; it is not innately emotional like humans. Furthermore, what if that data is biased? What if it has missing data? What if it is missing context? If we just run with AI, we can make incorrect, biased decisions.

Data and AI are valuable pieces for us to utilize in engineering intelligence, helping with decision making, but they are not the be all and end all. Engineered Intelligence means we are combining human skills with data and AI. Utilize data and AI with your IQ and EQ to make smarter decisions. This is why developing our data and AI skills matters. This way, we can interpret and understand the data and AI so we can understand how it fits into the context. We can understand how people will react to things when data and AI are used for decisions.

For example, imagine the data points in the direction of executing a new sales approach with a client that includes an expansion of the current product range. The data is showing that, but you know the company just launched a new product that is not doing too well. This may not be the right time to launch a sales push for expansion at the client. If one does not investigate, doesn't pay attention to what people are thinking, and just follows the data, then it may have a negative impact on the organization going forward and you may hurt a relationship with a client, hindering expansion in the future. This impact may be bigger than waiting to do the sales expansion for a year or however long, even if it means not hitting the revenue target with that company. Instead, people should be exploring the human side, the context side, so that decisions are made in intelligent ways.

In this chapter, we want to apply your human and emotional intelligence to data and AI decisions. We will be covering:

- a framework for you to use IQ and EQ for data and AI driven decisions
- a framework for you to use IQ and EQ for data and AI storytelling
- key tips, tricks, and change management with IQ and EQ with data and AI

These insights will help you develop personal skills that you can take forward to empower you in your data and AI driven decisions.

IQ and EQ: How Can We Improve in Data and AI Driven Decisions?

After the end of this section, I want you to thrive with your personal IQ and EQ, with ideas of how you can grow yours, within data and AI driven decisions. Let us start with IQ.

I want you to view your own personal IQ as the third leg of a stool for data and AI driven decisions. What I mean by this is that IQ plays a critical role in your personal data and information success, just like data and AI does. Your IQ represents your personal data points to add to a decision. You may be wondering what personal data points could be.

Imagine you are a salesperson working with a longstanding client, and the technical data shows that you should be pushing a large upgrade to a specific software and the organization is financially ready to deploy this. The problem the technical data has is missing information regarding what is going on in the business currently. You, on the other hand, utilize your IQ, knowing from your conversations with the organization that they are deploying a different, company-wide software update right now, and if you were to come in and propose the upgrade from your organization's software, it will probably be shot down because they are working on something big already. So, instead, you work to partner with them and help them deploy their current plans and then, when the time is right, you offer your upgrade to the other specific software.

Personal data points may be seen as less important or not as valuable as technical data points, but the reality is that sometimes the human personal data points matter just as much, or even more. We need to develop our ability and skills to combine the two, so we can make good decisions. So, don't discount your personal experience, ideas, and/or intuition.

Let's look at an example of data, AI, and IQ working together.

EXAMPLE

You have worked for the same company for 15 years. This company is building a new location for a store in the city you have helped to deploy one in before. You know the other store is across town, but will still have to play by the same rules to get the build approved and the contracts signed.

As the process is going along, the data is missing a key element that you remember from the last time a site was built: the contract duration. You look at the timeline for putting the building in place, when contracts are going to be sought for signature, and you notice the timeline is going to be off. This is a problem because the regional president is excited and wants to announce a kickoff for the site for the locals. If the regional president is going to kick off the site at the time they are proposing, you know it may run into a problem: the site may not be finished.

You go to your data analyst team or team that could have the contract data and ask where the data is on duration of contract signing. The team says we don't have that data. The data you requested was produced at a time when that data was not kept and recorded. You, with your personal experience, tell them the duration of time it took previously, and that you will talk to the city council to find out if the process has changed. You end up talking to the council and in fact the process is taking longer because of a backlog. You now have your personal data to add to the actual data and AI.

You present this to the team, help them understand the context, and help to ensure there isn't a problem for when the site launches.

Knowing your personal experience and ideas can be part of the conversation can help you develop confidence and skills with data. Does this mean they will always be very advantageous to the project? No, it doesn't, but it does mean they are a part of the conversation.

Remember, the three parts: IQ, data, and AI as the legs of a stool. Would you want to sit on a stool that has one, two, or three legs broken? I don't think you would. But remember that you want to include your personal data, your IQ, with the (let's call it) "technical" data and AI.

But now you may be asking, "What does EQ have to do with any of this?"

Emotional intelligence plays a part in our data and AI work. Now, we are going to expand the stool to four legs: data, AI, IQ, and EQ. This should look familiar: it is the formula:

Data + AI + IQ + EQ = Engineered Intelligence

By adding emotional intelligence, we are bringing unique elements that are personal and may help us to stand out. Having the ability to read the room, to understand how decisions will impact a team, and how things may work going forward is a great skill to have. We now have a stool with four legs on it. The same scenario applies: do you want to sit on a stool with one, two, three or four broken legs? I am not sure you would. So, strengthening the foundation of our chair can help us to build confidence going forward, allowing us to not only succeed but thrive through our work.

Let us jump into the first framework to incorporate IQ and EQ into our data and AI driven decisions. Remember, it isn't an all or nothing initiative we are looking at with data and AI, but an augmentation.

Your Engineered Intelligence Framework

Let's build an Engineered Intelligence framework that allows you to incorporate your personal data (IQ) and emotional intelligence to the table. One key word through this that I want to highlight is "augmentation" or "augmenting." Don't think you are being overrun or superseded by the technical, and forget the human element. You also may hear the term "human-in-the-loop." We are augmenting the human with the data and AI, and we are augmenting the data and AI with the human.

By thinking of our world as being augmented by data and AI, we can view it as like having a PhD-level partner at our fingertips to help us thrive.

> TIP
>
> Please understand that not all decisions you make with data, AI, IQ, and EQ will be big decisions. They can be small and still effective and impactful: sometimes, quick, easy decisions are enough. This can be key for you to understand because we may think we need to use all four elements to make a decision. That is not the case. You may just need one data point, like the weather forecasts for a business trip. Become confident and develop the skill to find where and when to use different parts of the equation and make engineering intelligence a part of what you do.

Framework Steps

You don't have to use every piece of this framework every time you make a decision. Instead, build confidence and skills that you can habitually use to make more intelligent decisions with data and AI. Why would I say you don't have to use every piece of the framework? This is because each of us is our own individual and there may be pieces here that you don't need to utilize. So, ensure you craft your own framework, using my steps or any others that you come up with that you find helpful. You can add in "blocking time off on your calendar," for example.

Here are the pieces of your framework:

- Determine your objective—What do you want to accomplish? You can use AI to help with this step to get going.
- Gather data—This is all data: human intelligence, emotional intelligence, the technical data, and AI (prompt responses, predictive analytics, etc.)
  - Don't forget to add in applicability—find areas where this makes sense in a real-world example to you.
- Remember the three Cs: flex your curiosity muscle, create, and think critically about the data.
- Ensure unbiased and fair data and AI work—work through the human emotions that empower the decision to be ethical, unbiased, and fair.
- Process and proceed with your decision—make decisions and evaluate them.

Below, we will now go through each of these steps in more detail.

Determine Your Objective

One thing that may hinder someone from making more inspired and powerful data and AI driven decisions is knowing just where to start, because there is so much information out there. One thing you can actually do is ask AI where to start. Below, I have an example of doing just that with Google's Gemini.
Prompt:

> "Hi Gemini, how are you today? I am looking to make an important career decision but don't know where to start, but I know I want to use data and AI to help. The decision is to help me advance in my skillset to help me move on to the next phase of my career. Right now, I work in marketing and want to lead a marketing team and not just be an individual contributor. How can I use data and AI to help me with the decision of how to proceed with my career to make this goal of leading a marketing team happen?"

When I used the prompt above, Gemini broke things down for me into phases. Phase 1 was data collection and self-assessment, Phase 2 was strategic planning and learning pathways, and Phase 3 was decision-making and action planning.

A phased approach is a great way to drive forward with a response, but remember that you are a key element to this. Over time, AI can learn more about you so can improve its responses, but at the same time it needs your creativity and ability to prompt it to get a good response.

How could we revise a prompt to do better than the above? Let me iterate on my prompt to make it more powerful.

Prompt 2:

> "Hi Gemini, how are you today? I am looking forward to moving on to the next phase of my career, but don't know where to start. I am currently a project manager in marketing, trained and certified, but I have used more of my knowledge and experience versus data and AI when I work. I know I want to use data and AI to help but don't know where to start. I am an eager learner and one who likes to have books and read. Right now, I work in marketing and want to lead a marketing team. How can I use data and AI to help me decide how to proceed with my career to make this goal of leading a marketing team real? What leadership and communication skills should I develop? How long should I plan for this first learning roadmap to be? What milestones can I put in the roadmap to help me succeed?"

You can easily prompt a different AI platform to gain a similar response. Now, it is up to you to do something with this response. With AI literacy (as discussed in Chapter 4), there are three steps: prompting, evaluating the prompt, and making a decision with it. Sometimes, that decision might be doing nothing and waiting. Sometimes, it might be directly getting to work on what you learned from the AI. You need to ensure you are prompting it and then utilizing the power of Engineered Intelligence that is at your fingertips.

Now, one thing that can help here is if you already have a system in place to get things done. Could you extrapolate ways from this system to empower you in your decision? This could be acting on the AI prompt response you received. It could be reworking the prompt and moving forward with this new one. Maybe there is a way you operate in a systematic forum in your daily work. The importance of having a daily routine was discussed earlier in this book. For example, time-blocking your calendar for 30 minutes each day to practice making decisions from responses from AI. It could also be adding AI to your daily workflow and operations—for example, using it to draft emails for you.

Gather Data

Now that we know our objective and have a plan or routine to implement it, it is time to gather the data to help you with this decision. A lot of times, we may think "data" means technical activities, such as using Excel. What if instead we start with our personal stories and data, the things that relate to us? Also, what if we decide to use those in combination with generative AI?

Let's use an example to help us.

EXAMPLE

Imagine you are working on a new marketing campaign, and the team asks you to make this one the best one they have had. As you start to study what they are trying to do, you notice a similarity to a marketing campaign that you did at a previous company. You don't remember every detail, but you do remember there were three key things that made it operate: the appropriate channel targeted social media campaigns, short burst videos were created, and the campaign had a duration of one month. As you share this with the organization, you then share the idea that these worked then, but it was two years ago, so it would be important to also gather data on the industry and the trends that are working now. With the pace of change occurring in the AI space, it may seem like it can be month-to-month on how things advance. That is okay, do you know why? Because you can focus on value and use cases and not worry about the rapid pace of change.

Once you have gathered the data, you then look at both and find that the three items from before still ring true, but there is one more key element that the data shows will matter to the campaign: social impact of the thing you are marketing. This is fantastic, you have gathered data to help with the decision, but what about AI?

Well, you decide to then prompt AI. I am going to give a sample prompt here:

> "I am working on a marketing campaign that we want to be innovative and impactful. I worked on a campaign in the past that worked well and had three main components to drive it forward: using social media as the channel for success, making the videos short, and having a campaign duration of one month. On top of this, recent data shows we need to ensure we are taking social impact into consideration. Can you craft an outline of further data we could use to make this marketing campaign positively impactful for us and our business?"

Here, the AI may lead us down a new path and help us gather even more data.

Please do not forget the use of personal data (human intelligence) in your analysis and decisions. This may mean bringing in a personal example outside of the business world, such as knowing how a specific demographic may positively react, and that is wonderful, do it. When we can apply things to our own life or real-world examples, we may get more people excited about the work.

Flex Your Curiosity Muscle

We know that over-reliance on data and AI may weaken our cognitive muscle. To ensure that this doesn't happen, we can work out our critical thinking and curiosity muscles, a key part of human intelligence. Remember, this involves asking questions—and lots of them. You may be asking yourself: What questions do I ask? Well, let's use AI as our friend to help you create a list.
Prompt:

> "I want to improve my curiosity and critical thinking skills. When making data and AI driven decisions, can you please create a list of 20 questions that will spark innovation, imagination, creativity, and help me with my data and AI driven decisions?"

Go ahead and try this, see what it comes up with. Here are a couple of the questions I received from the prompt:

- Beyond the obvious metrics, what unconventional data points could offer novel insights into this problem?
- If this AI model were a character in a story, what would its strengths, weaknesses, and potential "blind spots" be?

How could I improve the prompt above? Look at this iterated version:

> "I want to improve my curiosity and critical thinking skills. I feel these are valuable skills to have within a career. I also like to bring my personal interests, rugby and golf, into how I bring things to life. Please create a list of 20 questions related to these activities that will spark innovation, imagination, creativity, and help me with data and AI driven decisions. Thank you."

Now, these are ideas to get you going, but don't just rely on the AI for questions. Allow it to be your PhD partner, so we engineer intelligence and improve along the way. Allow it to help you generate ideas and help you succeed. Don't let it be everything you need.

Ensure Unbiased and Fair Data and AI Work

One thing we need to remember with data and AI work is that it can be biased, unfair, and unethical. We as humans can oversee this work to understand if the work is biased or unfair.

Datasets and AI models are only good as the data they are built with. If the data itself has issues within it, then we may struggle to get clarity and responses that are fair and equitable. For example, think about the banking and financial industry. You can have years of acquired data within the data, but what if during those years there were practices or policies that discriminated against some demographic? That data is then used to train the AI to make decisions, helping efficiency and maybe even automating those decisions.

If we don't examine these decisions, if we don't see how the AI is making them, the discrimination can be perpetuated. If the new data then feeds the model, a continuous cycle of discrimination may exist.

Now, you may ask how can I check for biases? What questions can I ask? I recommend the following questions:

1 Does this response actually make sense? If the response doesn't make sense, dig in and figure out why. For example, you may find the data is very skewed in one direction, which you were not expecting.
2 Get an accountability partner. This can be a good way to find if there are biases and things in place that are making the response not fair and equitable. Ask someone who isn't a part of your usual working group to read over the results and see if they make sense to them too. If they see issues, then dig into them.
3 How else can I view this data and analysis? Don't just take the first results you receive: do a second analysis, view the data in a new light and see if the results vary. We can get caught up in what is produced first and anchor on it.
4 Can I apply fairness metrics to assess the AI model's performance?

We can also ask AI for ways to check our data is fair and unbiased using a prompt such as the one below.
Prompt:

> "I am utilizing data and AI to help me with a decision, but I want to ensure it is clean and clear from biases and issues. Can you give me 10 ways to evaluate data and AI to help me understand if it is biased or unfair?"

Let's dive in with some ideas here for you. We looked at the example earlier of a financial institution having biased data that is then feeding the model and producing outputs that hinder decisions. Another example might be facial recognition where it is discriminating against people that look a certain way. What can be done here?

First, you should question everything. Use your own gut feel and personal data points on this. Don't just assume the outputs from an AI and data model are accurate because the technology said so. Instead, question it all, check for sources, do a double check. It doesn't mean you need to conduct a full-fledged analysis, but you should evaluate the work. Remember our point from above—another thing you can do is get others in your organization to analyze the results. It is one thing to have your personal input or ideas, but another if you get one or two more people on it.

Thirdly, do regular audits on the data feeding the models. Set aside maybe a day each quarter to evaluate the data and models. Run random prompts into the AI or conduct random audits within the data to see if it is operating in a way that is unbiased and fair.

Process and Proceed with Your Decision

The final piece of this puzzle with applying your IQ and EQ to making decisions is to actually make the decision and proceed forward. This may seem pretty simple and straightforward, but in reality we may have many ideas and things we want to get done, and some of these don't bring value.

So, what I want you to do as you read this is to commit to executing decisions, the ones that you believe are likely to be impactful. Experiment and roll with things. If it doesn't work out, no big deal. Instead, learn from it and continue.

A Framework for IQ and EQ in Data and AI Storytelling

Let's now jump into how to use your IQ and EQ for storytelling. For this section, I am not going to focus on the ways to tell stories with data and AI. Plenty of articles and books have been written on that, and so you can turn to existing resources, like Brent Dyke's book *Effective Data Storytelling*.[1]

Instead, I want to provide a reminder of the human skills that the World Economic Forum mentions as the fastest growing skills in 2030:[2]

1 AI and big data
2 networks and cybersecurity
3 technological literacy
4 creative thinking

5. resilience, flexibility, and agility
6. curiosity and lifelong learning
7. leadership and social influence
8. talent management
9. analytical thinking
10. environmental stewardship

Although it is probably not a surprise that AI and big data are at the top, look at the numbers that are human related: 3, 4, 5, 6, 7, 9. This is more than half of the list! For our purposes, we are now going to focus on these human elements attached to storytelling.

Technological Literacy

Just how should we define technological literacy? Is this that everyone knows the technical ins and outs of all things data and AI? Or will this work along the lines of data literacy: reading, working with, analyzing, and communicating with data?

Let us think of it in the same way that you would data literacy. We don't need everyone to get all in on the technical side of all things data and AI. Instead, they should get comfortable with the more accessible parts of data and AI, such as reading data or prompting AI models that are easier to learn. Think of data and AI like a smartphone. Do you know all the ins and outs of your smartphone? Do you know how the intricate details work together to bring you the experience you have today? Probably not, but you know how to use it to get your desired outcome, such as phoning, texting, or setting alarms.

Do the same with data and AI. You don't know all the ins and outs: instead, work to be comfortable with understanding the technology and then how to use it to bring value.

Creative Thinking

This is a key one for me. With data literacy, I had my three Cs: curiosity, creativity, and critical thinking. In the World Economic Forum list you have "creative thinking," but you also have "curiosity and lifelong learning" and "analytical thinking." How can we define creative thinking? Ask yourself this: who do you think are the most creative people? Children. Children go at things, figure things out, ask questions, and are creative. They can take a stick and make it a lightsaber or a sword. That's great! But what has happened to us as adults?

Now, I am not saying you can just go run and find a stick and sword fight with someone, but can we bring a bit of creativity to our lives with data and AI? If we are over-reliant on data and AI, our cognitive muscles can grow weak. Instead, why don't we bring new ideas to our prompts and uses of data and AI to solve our pain points? Go and try this, try thinking differently. Try to bring unique ideas and think big.

Resilience, Flexibility, and Agility

Resilience, flexibility, and agility are key skills for data and AI confidence because with the pace of change that we may experience—the advancements, the buzz, hype, and excitement—our ability to pivot, stand strong, and be resilient will be a powerful thing for us. My suggestions to help become more resilient, flexible, and agile are as follows:

- Develop knowledge by studying and continuously learning.
- Time-block your calendar for times of reflection, learning, and development.
- Craft stories around the updates and advancements of data and AI.
- Be curious, ask question after question, and then learn from the answers.
- Be optimistic and have a growth mindset which will improve your confidence as well as your skills.

Curiosity and Lifelong Learning

Although you will improve your confidence with data and AI, there is not a final point when we can stop learning and improving our skills. If we think we have arrived at a final point, we may lose ground and things pass us by. Instead, work to be a lifelong learner and lifelong question asker.

Leadership and Social Influence

Whether you are a leader by title or not, you can lead by example in your EQ and human skills.

Social influence is another that you may not feel is in your wheelhouse. However, instead of thinking you need to be the most extroverted person in meetings, or go to every work event, create influence by example. For example, share what you have learnt with your colleagues and teach them how you use it in your weekly team meeting. Share what is working and what isn't. This is part of being a helpful leader for your friends and colleagues.

Analytical Thinking

Analytical (and critical) thinking is a theme which is covered in many books—specifically on how to analyze data. So, we don't need to dive into all these different ways to think critically or analytically here. In fact, you can be a lifelong learner and dive into these topics while studying this book or afterward. But what I will say here is don't over-rely on data and AI. Instead, block your calendar and time for practicing critical thinking. Ask lots of questions, dig into the data, and, when needed, collaborate and work with others.

Conclusion

Developing skills and confidence in data and AI can be a challenge. People can worry about what skills they may possess, if any. That's okay, we don't need to have extensive knowledge of data and AI. Instead, I want you to focus on how your IQ and EQ, your personal skills, can empower you to have confidence. Find areas where you want to strengthen your skills, and find areas you want to say "You know what, I don't need to know that." Over time, you may find your niche in data and AI and thrive. Be that lifelong learner and be curious.

KEY TAKEAWAYS

- Your IQ and EQ matter and should be a part of your data and AI driven decisions.
- Be curious and a lifelong learner, so you can ensure you are growing and learning as technology advances.
- Use a framework to help you make decisions, but make the framework your own.
- Ensure your work isn't biased and it is ethical.

Notes

1 B. Dykes (2019) *Effective Data Storytelling: How to Drive Change with Data, Narrative and Visuals*, John Wiley and Sons, Inc., Hoboken, NJ

2 World Economic Forum. Future of Jobs Report 2025: 78 Million New Job Opportunities by 2030 but Urgent Upskilling Needed to Prepare Workforces, January 7, 2025. www.weforum.org/press/2025/01/future-of-jobs-report-2025-78-million-new-job-opportunities-by-2030-but-urgent-upskilling-needed-to-prepare-workforces/ (archived at https://perma.cc/G3FS-PJ5Y)

9

Talking the Language of Data and AI

Have you ever been in conversation with someone who is speaking the same language as you, but you have no idea what they are talking about? How confident are you in that conversation? Communication is such a vital part of our life, and it is the same with data and AI. Knowing what you don't know helps you to communicate more with those that do know, and you can develop your skills moving forward.

The definition of data literacy is "the ability to read, work with, analyze, and communicate with data." I give credit to Qlik for my time there where we utilized an older definition, modified it, and derived this one. I say the most important characteristic within the definition is the ability to read data. The reason being, if you don't read it right, how do we do the other three characteristics correctly? That said, if "read" is the most important, then communicating with data is the secret sauce to its success. Communication, whether with AI or about AI, is key for you to really develop skills and confidence with both data and AI. How should we then improve this?

First and foremost, a list of definitions was provided in the Introduction for you to study. You can refer to those terms to develop your vocabulary. Don't forget to turn back to the Introduction for words and definitions but, also, utilize the power of generative AI and ask it for definitions of words and how things are applicable to you. Did you ever ask in math class: where will I ever use this? Well, don't walk away from data and AI and ask where you will ever use it. Find out. What if you find an area you never thought of before and it becomes a great part of your life? Go experiment and learn.

We Have the Terms, Now What?

You may have seen all the terms in the Introduction, so do you have to jump into everything right now and learn it quickly? No, you don't. Instead, let's progress in this chapter and review a few more things to help you with your skills and confidence when communicating with data and AI. We will discuss:

- The importance of both context and nuance. Context and nuance can play a important part within communication. If we just share data points or AI responses without these things, we may not get very far.
- How we can translate the technical to the non-technical. How many people want to learn all the technical terms possible? Probably not many of us. Instead, making things relatable to your own work can empower you to understand and learn.
- How you can avoid some common pitfalls within data communication. You don't need to be perfect, but understanding some pitfalls may help you advance your effective communication skills.
- The importance of practicing.

Context and Nuance

From a pure definition perspective, context is the situation or environment that surrounds a word, idea, or event, giving it clear meaning. Can you think of areas in your life where context matters a lot? I have five kids, and when they give me information about school that can be good or bad, do I have the context to know what is going on and why it matters? Context and nuance are powerful to narrative and communication. We don't want to miss out on items of importance in our communication because we leave out context. It could be one of the most important things when creating narratives and communicating.

Let's look at context from a more general business setting before I jump into it from the data perspective. If I am running a marketing campaign, the context would be the information around the campaign, such as the demographics targeted, the duration of the campaign, and the platform the messaging appears on.

Within communication, context is an important thing. In fact, it is part of my five Cs of data storytelling: context, creativity, clarity, consistency, and conciseness. Each of these is pretty straightforward, but through it all, context may be the most important because if we don't know the reasons for how we are communicating, then we may not be using the other four correctly.

TIP

If you are struggling to understand data, ask the person communicating it to provide the context around the scenario, situation, or whatever the reason is for presenting the data. This may open your mind to the scenario and reality of the data. It may also open up the communicator to realize that they don't understand the data enough.

The last two words of the definition provided above, "clear meaning," are key when working with data and AI. We need this to understand how to use data and AI and make decisions that align with the business and the world around us. Without context, we can run into a big problem, as we may make incorrect decisions without knowing this.

Let's take a look at a business example of context. Imagine you are trying to build a relationship with a potential client. They have expressed the need for a new data program and want to use your organization's product. However, the person tells you there is a timing problem. They tell you that right now, the organization is going through an executive management team switch, so it is unlikely that any purchase will be made until the new leadership is in place. This is context to help you understand how to approach the company. You don't want to march forward and suggest buying something right now. Instead, use this contextual data to help you establish a stronger relationship with the company.

Nuance, defined as a small degree of difference or detail, is an important consideration alongside context. Nuance aids our communication as we are able to vary it—either by bringing certain things to light, helping to empower the listener, or to ensure the listener understands. An example of nuance in business communication is bringing a client to life. If we just look at their financials, we may get a picture of how the company is performing, but do we understand the organization as a whole? Its culture, strategy, market, and industry? Nuance is a good way to learn how to communicate with others, considering these aspects.

The Five Cs of Data Storytelling

Context

Context, our first "C" of data storytelling, was covered above. Let us jump into the other four. Before we do, do not forget that some context is going to be derived from the tone of the person speaking or even body language. When I am speaking in front of a crowd, I am not sure what is going on in their heads and it can be hard to understand if they are enjoying the session I am delivering. That being said, I can look at the reaction from the crowd as I speak. I can see their faces, their body language, and I can work off of those reactions. I may find they are happy or sad. If they look bored, I may need to change my tone and way of speaking quickly. So, don't just think of context in the form of words, notice other things that can drive context for you to understand the communication more powerfully.

In my career, I may have been in meetings where the tone of the meeting is one of urgency, which is a type of context and one that may spark me to understand we need to get things done quickly. I may be in a meeting where the tone is one of joy or excitement, so I know that this meeting may be one where I can get excited, too. Context and nuance can empower you, the user, to be more successful in your communication. Also, don't forget to convey things through your body language and ways that aren't necessarily vocal or written.

Creativity

We must consider if we can make our communication creative. Building a data story requires creativity so that people can relate to it. Imagine a person communicating about data and AI with pure technical terminology and wanting their team to buy into the idea and use it. It is most likely not going to work. Instead, imagine a person having the ability to creatively tie the data and AI together with context and nuance, bringing it alive. Senior managers and leaders are more likely to approve the data or AI concept.

Think back to the last example we used. Imagine that the company going through an executive management change is struggling with some processes that your tool can fix. Instead of pushing the sale now, you get creative and advise them on the current software, helping them get the most out of it, until the time they purchase yours. You bring in examples of how to drive the current solution to value. You effectively communicate the story of how to get more out of the current program, plus help set up the future relationship.

One example of data storytelling and creativity that can come into play effectively is the visualizations used to simplify data. For example, imagine an organization that has utilized statistical modeling to help drive investment decisions. The models are effective but complicated. Because of this, you start to simplify the modeling into visualizations. Then, it is easier to communicate the story the models are showing.

Clarity

We also want clarity. How many of us have been in a conversation and just look at the person because we are unsure of what they are saying? Try not to be the reason someone is confused. Think of the statistical models and how comfortable you would be using them. Do you have a sound understanding of statistics and would it be fine to use them? If not, you can ask for clarity, and if you are the one communicating, you can ensure you are clear.

Let's continue our example of the potential client requiring a new data program who are changing their executive team. You want to ensure they have a solid understanding that you know it will be a future sale, and what the next steps will be when they are ready. You can then build a relationship with them because they are happy that you are not pushing them to buy the product now.

Consistency

It is important to keep the way you communicate consistent. It is not good if a company tries to sell a product to you by emailing for two weeks, then calling multiple times the next, then texting, and, finally, visiting the office.

Discuss with people internal and external to the business about the ways they like to be communicated with, and adhere to their preference on the frequency of these communications. By doing this, we can maintain a good working relationship.

Think of our example: you ask the client for their preferred method of communication and say that you will check in once a month via this method about the executive team switch so the conversation can move forward to a purchase.

Conciseness

The last "C" stands for conciseness. Provide the most important information to avoid overloading others because data and AI can become technical!

In our example, conciseness would help you not bother or annoy the potential client, especially because they are working through a big personnel shift within their company.

Within the work of data and AI, the ability to bring context to a scenario in the communication we have empowers both the listener and communicator. Plus, if one has the ability to bring nuance to the conversation, we are now in a position to help the listener understand or bring the scenario to light more powerfully. As you develop your confidence and skills within data and AI, work to get good at communicating context and understanding nuance. As you improve, drive forward not just with context and nuance, but with the five Cs. By getting good at communication, understanding the vocabulary and terminology, you can develop your confidence.

Translating the Technical to the Non-technical

The ability to translate technical language to non-technical language is a key skill which enables better understanding from the listener, increasing the likelihood that they come on board with the data and AI project. However, if we don't possess the technical knowledge and need to learn, what can we do? We start with the power of questions.

Ask Questions

Remember the five Cs above? You can actually utilize questions in relation to each of these to empower you to understand the technical aspects of data and AI. Ask yourself these questions to further your own understanding in your research, about data or AI implementation at work, or be prepared to answer these if you suggest a data or AI tool.

C1: Context:

- What is the purpose of the data and AI you are using?
- Can you tell me why you chose the analysis you did to arrive at the insight?
- How did you go about analyzing the data?
- Do you have an end goal or decision you want this data to help with?
- What is the problem statement you are working toward solving?
- How does this tie to the goals and objectives you are working on?
- What skills could I develop that would help me to be empowered to understand the context more fully or easily?

C2: Conciseness:

- That was a lot of information, can you break it down into simple steps for me?
- Can you share what your end goal was and what the decision you made was?
- That email was very long; how could I make it shorter for my readers next time?

- I think you have shared multiple points and ideas, but I am unclear which one I should focus on, can you make it more concise?
- From a self-reflection perspective: I built this analysis, but it may be a bit confusing for the end users to understand, what can I do to break this down? How can I empower my end users by bringing clarity to this and making it shorter? (Who wants to read a long, drawn-out memo or analysis? Who has time for it? Asking ourselves how we can improve our work to be more concise may help our colleagues to understand things better.)

C3: Creativity:

- This was a great analysis; how can this be applied to a real-world scenario?
- What are the most powerful ways I can visualize and drive understanding through creative dashboards and stories?
- Were there other ways you tried to analyze the data, and what made you think of these?
- How can we write this into a data story to help us to share it more clearly?
- I want to be different here, is there anything I can do to bring this to life more?

C4: Clarity:

- The message you are sharing isn't quite coming across, how could we simplify this?
- Are there any things we can take out of this to simplify it?
- If I were to read this, would this come across clearly and easily? If not, what can I do to make it better?
- Would I be able to understand this if I didn't know what the scenario was?
- Does my audience have the time for a longer explanation, or do they need to have a quick and easily understandable analysis?
- Did I pick the right communication channel to help drive success?

C5: Consistency:

- Which communication methods have I been using? Do these methods still make sense? Is my audience liking these methods, or do I need to adjust?
- How regularly have I been communicating with others?
- How did you build this dashboard, and how can we make sure we make dashboards like this going forward?

By utilizing these questions, you can help yourself or others as the communicator to be more effective and empowered. We don't want to lose the insight and power of data and AI because we aren't communicating well. I'd guess that 90 to 99 percent of data and AI success hinges on people, and our secret sauce to people using it more effectively can be the communication we use.

Simplify Terminology Where Possible and Utilize AI to Be Creative

Another way to improve our move from the technical to the non-technical is to receive help from AI. Here are a couple of prompts that show how you can ask an AI to simplify terminology. Remember to evaluate the response and make it your own.

Prompt 1:

> "I am working with my sales team to help them understand a new product that was built from studying the data around the market and with the help of AI. Unfortunately, the report that has come to me has lots of technical words and this isn't going to be how sales want to receive the information. I have attached the document here. Can you please go through it and rewrite this for me, so it is easier for non-data and non-AI people to understand? Also, outline for me how to make an effective presentation to them about the report. Please suggest what can go on the slides. Thank you."

Prompt 2:

> "I am not a data or AI professional, so I don't understand the technical terminology well. I just received information from our AI team to help

me with the marketing campaign I am working on. Unfortunately, there is a lot of technical terminology within it. Can you review the information for me and provide me with definitions for the technical terms? Then, rewrite the information in a non-technical manner that I can study and learn from? Thank you."

Another thing that could be impactful with AI is to generate new ideas or be innovative with the communication. Here is a prompt that you can use to bring creativity to the story or communication:

> "I am working on a project for my company. I feel the communication we are using is pretty dry and won't excite the audience. This makes me fearful that employees may struggle to buy in and may not want to take on the work this project will require. I have attached a document that covers the project, can you help me craft an innovative communication strategy? My company is a younger company, only five years old, and has 500 employees. We want this to thrive, and we want to make a splash with the project. Please help me to be creative and powerful."

Common Pitfalls and Mistakes

Poor communication can result in a loss of trust and ineffective decisions. Let's look at some common pitfalls that can get in our way, and how to overcome them:

1. **Utilizing technical jargon**—As we have discussed throughout this chapter, when the majority of people aren't data and AI professionals, using technical jargon may confuse them. If you are the communicator, look for ways to simplify the message and avoid the world of technical words where possible. If you need to use technical jargon, work to include explanations of what that term or word is.
2. **Using too many words**—There is an acronym: K.I.S.S. It means "keep it simple, stupid." However, Einstein is quoted as saying: "Make everything as simple as possible, but not simpler." Yes, we should simplify things, but don't oversimplify. We do not want to lose the message within by leaving things out that are crucial.

3 **Communicating in the way you like**—One key thing you can do to ruin communication is build communication channels that you like, but not the ones your colleagues would like. This means you need to get to know the audience. What do they understand? What are their data and AI literacy levels? You may think your communication is really strong and then find out that no one understood your points, or cared.
4 **Not utilizing the power of visualization**—Our most powerful sense, like touch or taste, is visual. We can help ourselves out by crafting good and useful visualizations that work for our audience. Not understanding our audience can hinder our ability to build poor communication.
5 **Not thinking about the narrative enough**—Narrative can empower our communications with data and AI. What are we trying to accomplish and why? By leaving out this narrative and "why," our audience may not be able to successfully adopt our changes.
6 **Leaving out IQ and EQ**—If we focus our communications solely or mostly on the data and AI, but we leave out the IQ and EQ (the human side), we may miss completely as people may feel they have been left out. Ensure you are taking IQ and EQ into the communication, so it has a human element.
7 **Crafting the email toward the technical and process, not toward the outcome and audience**—If we are focusing our communication on the data, the AI, and not the outcome, we may not help our audience know what is to be achieved with what we are doing. Yes, the data and AI matter, but the narrative matters more. Use data and AI to support the narrative, not be the narrative.

Overall, these are seven things to avoid. You may have also thought of other things you would want to avoid. Test things out, explore and experiment, figure things out. Find what works for you and roll with it. One thing you can do is ask AI how to overcome a pitfall you feel you have.

For example, one pitfall that can happen is in the building of the presentation itself. If we put too much information in a presentation slide, it can distract from the message when we present. Don't have too many words on the slides as it can take the listener away from

you and into the slide, missing important things you are saying. How can we prompt this?
Prompt:

> "I am a marketing assistant who is helping my team present our new AI strategy. I have attached a slide deck for you to review. I think the slides have too many words on them. I want to make these more concise, whilst keeping the important points. Thank you."

Practice, Practice, and Practice Some More

Overall, you will want to practice, but this doesn't just mean by communicating. A significant part of communication is active listening. Ensure you are listening for context and nuance and note down the terms you don't know. Active listening can help you to communicate better. You can hear when people are and aren't comfortable, understanding what your audience or those you are conversing with want.

Also, practice using the terms in the Introduction. Make it a habit to study a term each day. Write it down, work to use it in a sentence, and practice the skills around that word. If you are studying prompting and prompt engineering, then practice this while you study the definition.

Furthermore, immerse yourself in the language of data and AI and don't be embarrassed if you don't get it right. That may be easier said than done, but don't be afraid to try and use a term even if it falls flat. It is like trying to learn a new language in another country: as you practice the language over time, you will naturally develop skills and confidence in that language.

You could even prompt AI to derive a game that you can use to practice on a regular basis and commit the definitions to memory.

Be a student of the world of data and AI: practice and learn to develop your confidence and skills in this area. What can you do with AI to be a student of communication with data and AI? Here is a prompt:

> "I want to continue to learn different skills in communicating with data and AI, but I don't know where to start or begin. Please help

me to develop a learning path and plan to thrive with data and AI communication skills. For this learning path, please spell out what the most important terms are for a newcomer to data and AI. Please simplify the terminology for me and ensure it isn't explained in technical terms. Where you can, give examples for me to study with regard to the terms. Thank you for your help."

Non-verbal Communication

Non-verbal communication is a crucial part in effectively conveying data and AI messages. My career has required me to do a lot of public speaking and I have been able to go to various places around the world. As I am speaking on topics within data and AI, one thing I can do is notice if the audience is getting bored or not paying attention. If I notice these things, I need to be the one who responds. Maybe it is time for me to call a break or to ask a question, do something to get the interaction going in a direction that helps.

In the data and AI space, as you are working to develop confidence and skills, get good at recognizing non-verbal cues that help you succeed with data and AI. Don't just make it about the words you use, also look at the non-verbal cues you can pick up on.

Another thing you can focus on is the non-verbal skill of listening. You don't always talk in communication; you always need to listen to things. Actively listen so you know how to respond. Don't listen to respond. Listen to learn and then actively communicate from the learning.

Conclusion

Overall, communication is the secret sauce to data and AI success. There are lots of skills to learn, so don't stress if you don't have all the skills now. In fact, the journey to good communication skills can be a lifelong journey, as AI will continue to progress beyond what we know of it.

Don't focus on perfection or knowing everything. Instead, focus on these main questions: Can you ask the right questions about data and AI? Can you clearly articulate the insights from the data discovered? Can you communicate the decisions made from this and move forward? Can you shift technical language to become less technical, whether you use AI to help or not?

KEY TAKEAWAYS

- Don't forget the terms provided in the book's Introduction, utilize them and thrive.
- Communication isn't just speaking, but also active listening.
- Find ways you can increase your skills and improve your data storytelling.
- Be a student of the world of data and AI.

10

Build Better Value with Data and AI

Okay, let's start this chapter off with an assignment. I want you to pull out a journal or piece of paper as you read this chapter and take notes. What are your thoughts? What are you learning? Is there a topic you want to expand your knowledge on?

It goes without saying at this point that the world of data and AI can bring value to both individuals and organizations. Think about how data can help us make smarter decisions, instead of making guesses and hoping those turn out well. Think about how much effective use and understanding of AI can empower us. This book is focused on data and AI skills, to improve our confidence, and one thing that can help us to develop more confidence is to see the value it brings—not just some generated image or fun prompt you put in and it gives a good response. Real value to us, such as time freed up in our day-to-day role so we can then spend more time on more exciting projects, or new insight into a sales campaign or new product that helps you contribute to your team or even get promoted.

Another way to look at it in our careers is how we utilize data and AI to drive more productive and powerful meetings, whether internally for ourselves or for clients. These are things that can empower us to drive value using Engineered Intelligence.

Overall, data and AI represent power to help us engineer intelligence and can help us in our lives, but if we aren't deriving value from data and AI, why would we use it? It would be like purchasing a piece of gym equipment for a specific fitness goal, but not knowing how to use it and therefore not getting the intended impact from it.

In this chapter, we will explore the following:

- What does it mean to derive value from data and AI?
- A framework to evaluate and derive value from data and AI.
- Where human thought, emotion, intuition, and gut feel come in.

We will also discuss what is actually possible for individuals and organizations. Ultimately, deriving value from data and AI where we have not been using it before means we need to transform and innovate. "Transformation" can be an overused buzzword, so we will explore what it actually means and how we can tie it to value from data and AI.

Value from Data and AI

To help us understand how to derive better value from data and AI, let's make sure we have a solid understanding of what we mean when we say value. Value does not necessarily have to be monetary, or tangible. Think of relationships with friends and family, for example, and how much value they can bring to your life. Also, think back to Chapter 5; learning was discussed as something of value. Therefore, we can define value as something of worth.

So, when we think of data and AI, we can say that value from data and AI means it is producing something of worth. What could that be? Let's take some examples to help frame this for us.

Example 1: Use AI to Set Goals and Create Plans

You can utilize AI as your partner to help you set goals that move you forward in your career. When I turned 43 years old, which happened when I was writing this book, I used AI to set goals for the year. One of these goals focused on my career in AI: that I will be a world leader of strategic knowledge and vision in AI by my birthday in 2026. The AI then went on to help break this down into phases and milestones. What a great way to utilize AI to help us all achieve career goals and build ways to accomplish this.

Maybe you are looking to develop into a marketing leader that utilizes data and AI. AI can help you to set a plan that takes you to where you want to be. An example prompt for this could be:

> "I am a marketing manager who has been in the space for a few years. I have succeeded with my goals and aspirations as a manager, but feel I could lead a larger team. I have read some books but don't feel they are clear enough to get me where I want to go. Can you please provide me with some goals to work toward within marketing that will take me from a marketing manager to a director or vice president level? Please include the skills that could be needed to jump from one career progression to another. Thanks for your help."

Another example prompt is provided below:

> "I am trying to think of multiple examples of where I can derive value from data and AI. I am in sales at an industrial supply company. I want to use data and AI to propel me forward to my sales goals and metrics, plus help me to understand the clients better. This can help me to understand data and AI more and build confidence in using data and AI. Can you not only show me different examples of using data and AI to derive value either in a sales career in industrial supply, but can you help me to see what skills I may need to develop to ensure I find value? Thank you for your help."

> TIP
>
> The prompt response can be as valuable as you make it. It could tell you things you already knew, so you iterate the prompt and make it better, or things you did not even know existed and so you iterate it more to learn about those specific topics. It may have given you things you had been thinking about, but did not feel assured could bring you value.

Example 2: Now That You Have Your Goal, Use Data and AI to Propel You Further Toward It

Using data and AI to help one in their career may take on different faces for different people. One may use data in their day-to-day job that empowers them to make better decisions overall. Another may use data and machine learning for predictive analytics that help them propel forward with success. For instance, let's return to our marketing leader example: you could use predictive analytics to decide which demographic is going to be more accepting of a new marketing campaign or predict what kind of marketing should be done to grab people's attention. As you become comfortable with skills to deploy predictive analytics, it becomes a key thing you bring to the table, distinguishing yourself and potentially providing opportunities to take on new responsibilities.

Overall, hopefully, you are seeing more of the value and ability of data and AI to bring value to your career, but one of the keys here is to have the skills to do it. It is one thing to talk about and another to help you build confidence and skills to actually succeed. Let's jump into this in the next part of this chapter.

Data and AI Skills for Value

Now, let us think about how to develop skills, including those you may receive from a prompt response.

Curiosity

Curiosity has appeared throughout this book. How do curiosity and asking questions come into play with value? This is because curiosity can be a catalyst, causing a reaction to take place for you within data and AI. Curiosity as a catalyst is a way for us to unlock doors to ways of doing things, goal setting, and generating value in different ways. Then, we allow our curiosity to drive us forward.

As we have mentioned previously, to become curious we need to ask more questions. Here are some questions you can ask to derive value from data and AI:

- How does this data tie to the business goals?
- What can I do with AI for this specific project?
- Are we measuring the right things?

- What will the outcome of this project look like, and does that provide value to the organization?
- Why am I working on this? (If we don't know why we are working on something, then we may focus on things that aren't going to provide value.)

These don't represent all the possible questions, but use these as a starting point. Create a list of curiosity questions and use them to spark your data and AI work.

Think of curiosity in your career to be like searching for and finding a pot of gold at the end of a rainbow. It could be that you have seen rainbows over and over again in your life, like spotting a trend or pattern in your career. You then become curious: what does this trend or pattern mean? Can data and AI make sense of this and help you find value?

Finding the pot of gold could mean digging into data more or discussing your idea with more advanced data and AI professionals, as this could be a problem they can help you solve.

The "Why"

One skill you can develop is keeping your eye on the prize, the "why." The why is understanding what you are doing with data and AI in relation to business goals. Your work must align with your organization's goals and objectives, so learn those first—especially because this will improve buy-in from senior personnel if you want to implement a specific data or AI tool!

How many times have we done something without knowing the why and really believed in it? We buy into a solution more when we understand the why. Now think of a time when you were excited about something and believed in the "why." It can be a difference that impacts the effort you bring to work, which can have a large impact on value.

Now, let's turn back to our prompting to give you an idea of how to focus on the "why." I input the following prompt into Gemini:

> "I really want to improve my ability to focus on the 'why' of my data and AI work. Can you help me understand how to get to the 'why' of

work, and also a framework on how to refocus if distraction kicks in? Thanks."

The prompt response provided some points that I have summarized here.

1. START WITH THE END IN MIND

If you can clearly see the end goal in mind, you can see the value and "why" that can be derived from the work. To picture the end goal, turn away from the distractions you may have, like your computer or phone. With this in mind, time-blocking is something we will speak more about below. Get in a room and write down ideas about what the end goal might look like. Then, work backwards to get there, figuring out data points you may need or AI solutions you can use. Utilize the end goal to help you see the path.

2. ASK "WHY" REPEATEDLY

When you receive some data and it tells you something, ask why? If you then get an answer there, ask why again... and again... and again. It may be that you go down a path that is very different than the path you set out on originally and that is okay. We need flexibility and agility (remember it's one of the fastest growing skills by 2030!).

3. DEFINE SUCCESS METRICS

If we have a "why," what does success look like? Do we know and understand the metrics that will get us to our end goal over time? How we define success can vary. For example, with AI, it is a new world and so using traditional success metrics may not empower us as much as we need. So, we can look to define success differently, such as how impactful a meeting was because we utilized data and AI to make it more impactful. We can look at the value we derive from a presentation because it was designed more powerfully. Metrics can be defined by you, and you can even ask AI: how should I define success for this goal?

Then, after you have hit that goal, you keep going. You iterate and do more. You may have found a new goal to move toward, but don't stop and think you have a finish line. Then, we work to set new success metrics as we can have new goals and targets. The metrics of success continually evolve, and we continually work toward progress and success. An important thing to note is that success doesn't have to be a monumental thing. Small successful steps work, too.

4. VISUALIZE THE IMPACT

If you can't see success at the end, then why would you do the work or project? Visualize what success with the project looks like. What are people saying about the project? How is it being received? Is it even being received at all?

5. COMMUNICATE AND VALIDATE

Don't just determine a "why" on your own, get stakeholders and champions involved. Validate your thoughts through success metrics, and be open for feedback. Validate metrics and success, pivot and iterate where you need, and then bring success to the project. How do we validate metrics and success? We need to not work on this individually. Ask others if the metrics make sense, ask them if what we see in the data is working and successful. Don't just use your own mind for this. Instead, ask others and work with them on metrics and success.

Time-Blocking

Time-blocking is "a time management method where you divide your day into blocks of time. Each block is dedicated to a specific task or group of tasks."[1] Why does time-blocking matter to deriving value from data and AI? We live in an era where we can get distracted. Teenagers can focus on a task for 90 seconds, and adults are not much better, with a focus time of three minutes.[2]

We may have work responsibilities that are very time-consuming, and so being able to focus on your work is hard. We have distractions at our fingertips, like doomscrolling social media. We have Teams or Slack messages hitting us frequently, so we have to context switch. We may be distracted more than we realize.

Ask yourself these questions:

- Do you feel like you are getting the most out of your work?
- How many things are you currently working on that you feel are a waste of time? Do you feel they could be done better?
- How much time do you have to do focused work each day?
- How much time do you have each week for personal development?

These are questions you can ask and where time-blocking can help you dedicate availability for focused work and personal development. Time-block your calendar for specific data and AI tasks and fill your calendar up. You can block time for yourself to reflect and think, without distractions. This can enable you to think deeper about a problem you are trying to solve. It could be that it enables you to not have to context switch between work problems and your data and AI initiative.

For example, imagine you are working on an important PowerPoint presentation, and you have multiple people contacting you via Slack or email. Each time you see a notification, you stop and read it. Then, you have to remember where you were in the presentation and have lost a good thought. Have you ever asked "Where was I?" or "What was I going to do here?"

Time-blocking allows you to not have these distractions get in the way of your work. Instead, you are focused and getting possibly your best work done.

We can also time-block for personal development. If you want to develop your confidence and skills in data and AI, you will need to set aside dedicated time to be able to read, study, and learn. So, time-block that into your calendar and develop your career.

Furthermore, time-blocking can help to avoid burnout. When I was helping to build the concept of data literacy, I was very busy traveling the world for speaking engagements, but my body was not responding to it well and I did not know it. So, it eventually caused burnout, and I became depressed. Time-blocking could have empowered me to take more breaks and reflect on my activity levels more, meaning I could have been healthier. I could have concentrated more on the most important parts of the work instead of everything. Use time-blocking to your advantage to do better work and empower your health.

Domain Knowledge

Domain knowledge is a foundational data and AI skill. This does not suggest that you need to be an expert in data and AI but ask yourself: what are you an expert in, or what interests you? You may not think you are an "expert" in something, but you have knowledge and ideas. Do not sell yourself short. What are you good at? Which topics interest you? What would you like to become more knowledgeable about? Applying your ideas and knowledge with data and AI can be how to obtain the value you want.

In a business setting, where do you have domain knowledge? Do you have a strong understanding of B2B marketing? Are you good at building products? What does your domain knowledge do for you to strengthen your work with data and AI? Take your domain knowledge and make it a superhero strength for yourself to help you engineer intelligence. I love to study philosophy and think deeply. How can I apply that to business? Are there philosophies I can bring to my prompting and business ideas? I like reflection and deep thinking. Can I apply that to prompt responses to derive more effective decisions? For example, if we just rush through things on building a new marketing campaign or a new product and don't take time to reflect on what we are doing, could we build something that doesn't work or isn't what it could have been? Take time to reflect on the work itself.

You may have studied for a specific degree that did not cover data or AI in any way. However, the skills you learnt can still help with data and AI. Take an art history degree, for example. As an art history student, you were able to see the stories within the paintings, the reaction to that point in time. This applies to data and AI in the way that being creative improves data literacy, and that data storytelling is essential for. Are you asking why storytelling matters here? Because stories bring things to life. Data is just data, and it sits there. Analytics can be great for insight, but the story brings it to life and can help apply things to applicable situations. Don't miss out on the power that communication and stories can bring.

Don't think because you didn't go to school to study data and/or AI that you don't have domain knowledge that helps you contribute in a meaningful way, or that you can't develop it. You may just need to think about it deeper.

Technical Skills

Now, don't worry, when I say "technical skills." I am not saying you need to learn many difficult ones. However, it is useful to learn the basics about technical skills such as data analysis, statistics, or coding. Now, you don't need to build coding for advanced statistical analysis, but you could learn the terminology. Then, you can work with the technical teams and communicate with them better.

If you don't know where to start or how to study technical skills, in the next section I will teach you how to prompt AI for a learning framework, including how to get started.

Data and AI Value Learning Framework

Let's teach you how to prompt for your own learning framework and then give you the results. That said, please know that you can modify the prompt and the framework itself.

Prompt:

> "I am looking to learn more data and AI skills and develop more confidence in these so I can create better value from data and AI. Can you please create a framework for developing more skills in data and AI so I can do this? Please include how I can get started when I am stuck and don't know how to proceed. Thank you."

Below is a framework that was derived from my prompt which I have summed up. This framework will help you develop your data and AI skills and derive better value, along with strategies for when you feel stuck.

The first phase of the framework covered foundational knowledge. The goal for this phase is to understand core concepts, language, and the potential of data and AI. The key skills and areas are around data literacy, AI fundamentals, business acumen, and problem solving. We discussed data literacy in Chapter 3 and AI literacy in Chapter 4. We looked at terminology in the Introduction. You can go back to these if you want to review them.

This phase also highlighted the importance of mindset, which we will talk about in Chapter 12. Your mindset should shift from one lacking in confidence toward data driven problem solving.

In Phase 2, the emphasis is on practical skills and tools for hands-on application, as we can't just learn theoretical things. These practical skills include programming, data acquisition and pre-processing, machine learning algorithms, and generative AI applications. It could also be analysis, finding ways to derive insight from data and information. It may be how to craft a data story utilizing a data visualization tool. It could be learning how to read data better. There are different skills you can learn, which are not inaccessible or extremely technical.

Phase 3 is value creation and strategic application. We have talked about value creation, but strategic application matters too. We don't want to put data or AI tools into our own hands or the hands of others, only to find out that we, or they, are not equipped to know how to apply them well. Key activities for this phase are a problem-first approach, use case identification, proof of concept (POC) and piloting, communication and storytelling, and ethical and responsible AI implementation.

Phase 4 is continuous learning and adaptation. We want to continuously learn and not become stagnant. We want to be flexible and adaptive. Don't just go with what's in front of you and don't think you have made it to the finish line. Be a lifelong learner.

Following this phase, it is important to stay up to date on trends. Now, does this mean knowing all the trends? It doesn't, that would be hard, but it does mean consistently learning. You can also deepen your specialization in this area. The world of data and AI is vast, so it may be hard to be an expert in everything. So, if you find an area you like, then develop in it. Also, from this phase you can experiment and build, and, finally, teach and share.

This framework will help guide you from a place of uncertainty and build your confidence phase by phase.

The Human Side: Gut Feel, Emotion, Experience, Intuition

In this era of AI, you can ask yourself: do I even fit in? What about my thoughts, ideas, gut feel, and experience? Am I going to be passed over? Remember, everyone has a place at the data and AI table. You have a place at the table. Building your data and AI skills will help you cut through the hype. Remember, the goal is to derive Engineered Intelligence with our formula. This can help us get to success. So, you do matter, and you don't need to get yourself caught up in the hype and buzzwords that are out there. Instead, lock in and focus to get what you can out of yourself, data, and AI.

With your IQ and EQ, we ensure that we are not forgetting to develop our cognitive muscles so that we do not lose our ability to think and apply the human side. Be a lifelong learner and continually develop. Using the frameworks provided in this book, you can continually develop.

However, one key to watch out for is that emotion isn't pulling you forward too much. Are we bringing in bias or emotion that can take a project off in a direction it shouldn't? Emotion can be good, but can guide us in ways we don't want. This can be not taking on data and AI work because we are fearful; we do not know what we are doing, so we ignore the trends. It can be we don't want to develop something with data and AI because it may render us redundant and so we hold off.

Instead of fearing these things, continue to develop your confidence and skills, helping the organization to deploy innovative and potentially transformative solutions.

The areas of gut feel, experience, intuition, whatever you want to call it, are personal data points from your emotional intelligence to add in. Remember, our formula is:

Data + AI + IQ + EQ = Engineered Intelligence

When we think of that world of Engineered Intelligence, we ensure we are a part of the equation, engineering new solutions or innovation. We sit in a time when AI can be a powerful resource for us, helping us to innovate and transform things. Don't get caught in the negative buzz and fear. Use your ideas and thoughts and apply them with data and AI. It is key to have enough IQ and EQ to recognize your ideas and thoughts that need to be superseded by data and AI. You also want to learn how to supersede your thoughts and ideas with data and AI. How can you do this? Well, experiment and test it. When you have a mindset to iterate and move yourself forward, you can learn and develop yourself.

Conclusion

Find confidence from the fact that data and AI can bring huge value for your career, so ensure you are working toward creating this value. Remember to make yourself a permanent part of your own success. Keep on developing your domain knowledge, your skills, your ideas. Learn to apply data to those ideas and learn how to use AI to your advantage. That is key to helping you find success.

Let's finish this chapter turning back to the assignment from the beginning of the chapter. Pull out your journal and review what you wrote down. How does it look? Are you feeling more confident in your data and AI skills?

KEY TAKEAWAYS

- Know how you are defining value for yourself with data and AI.
- Don't focus on proof of concept, but proof of value.
- The human side matters, so use it. Don't forget that your ideas and gut feel matter.
- Use and adapt the data and AI value learning framework.

Notes

1 L. Scroggs. Time Blocking, Todoist, www.todoist.com/productivity-methods/time-blocking#time-blocking-methods (archived at https://perma.cc/CHG2-3AGX)

2 J. Hari (2022) *Stolen Focus: Why You Can't Pay Attention – and How to Think Deeply Again*, Crown

11

Becoming a Data and AI Leader in Your Organization

The Power of Change Management

How many of us like the word "change?" Is this something you thrive with, or something that scares you away? Change is an interesting topic. Many people talk about change: the need for change, the ability to change, and our desire to change. When it comes down to it, though, we may not be the best at actually changing or sustaining the change.

One thing we don't want to have happen is to get caught up in "New Year's Resolution Syndrome," as discussed in Chapter 3. What happens when a new year comes along? People get excited and set resolutions to improve and get better. But, within a few weeks or months, they have fallen short of achieving the resolution they set. Is this because they didn't really want to achieve what they set out to? Probably not. They maybe really wanted it and went for it, but then they didn't sustain the change they set forward to accomplish. We don't want to get caught up in our work of trying to enact change, only to fall short and not achieve it.

The world of data and AI can involve rapid change. We may be hearing about new AI talk and discussions happening around us. This can cause us to worry and to lose confidence in our abilities, which of course is not what we want to happen. With changes in data and AI, we want to sustain the changes and additions we make. We don't want to fall short with our resolutions and work. Instead, we want to grow and thrive with the changes that will happen. We want the changes to be empowering. Instead of "change," it may be more helpful to use "evolve" or "transform."

The reality is, in the data and AI space, change management hasn't necessarily been thought about enough to help organizations to thrive with data and AI. In fact, it may be one of the most forgotten things within data and AI. Instead, the focus has been on the "shiny object" that is in front of the world, like generative AI or a data tool that may appear to solve a lot of problems. However, hearing about these different tools can be a problem.

One reason is because tools themselves aren't strategies. Tools are there to support a strategy, like a hammer is there to support the construction of a house. The hammer is not a strategy itself, but there to support it. With data and AI, tools aren't going to be adopted wholly without effort to integrate them into existing processes. Tools are something to help us move forward with change, like the hammer is a tool to build a house. I want to emphasize that data and AI are pieces that help build the house, whether a personal career path plan or new marketing campaign or even a new product. Allow data and AI to be a part of the journey to get us to the end product.

Data and AI tools are powerful, but if we jump into the world of data and AI without change management, it could be like jumping into a pool without being able to swim. Does that seem like an adventure we want to dive into? In this chapter, we will discuss:

- What is change management?
- Why does change management matter?
- A change management framework for you to use in your personal life and at work.

What Is Change Management?

Change management is an established and important part of business work. *Forbes* defines change management as "a structured process for planning and implementing new ways of operating within an organization."[1] Look at the words "planning" and "implementing."

We are working toward end goals, and it may be that we thrive more when we have planned the changes and effectively implement them.

So, how does change management play into data and AI work? Change management can be key to deploying data and AI work effectively, because data and AI work is often new and can alter the way things are done in a business; sometimes we alter things in a big way. As most professionals are not data and AI professionals, when a new process with data and/or AI is implemented, it can be a huge change for people and not one they wanted to have in the first place. The human element can make up a big portion of data and AI work. We may think of data and AI work as driven by the tech, but it will be humans implementing it. So, we want to manage the change appropriately.

Changes, from a new dashboard being built and shared to full tool deployment, need to be managed well and special care must be taken to ensure success and buy-in to the program. With that in mind, it becomes more important for a business to understand how a change is going to impact the business and how to get people on board whilst deploying and adopting a change. Again, just jumping in can have results we don't want, plus, when a financial investment has been made, it can mean a low ROI, if any.

On the other hand, when it is an effective, empowering change, we need to ensure the messaging around it highlights its effectiveness, so people understand what is going on. We also want to ensure we have a sustained change and not an overnight "big bang" that fizzles away over time. This is also a place for people to increase their data and AI literacy skills to effectively understand the data and AI work being accomplished.

Now, you may ask yourself: how can I prompt a generative AI model to empower me with more skills and confidence with data and AI work, or how can I use it to help me be empowered and not overwhelmed by the change? You can use any of the following yourself and see what results you receive. Remember, you don't have to use my exact wording; instead make it your own. Test out variations and experiment to empower your prompt skills and abilities with generative AI.

Prompt 1:

"Hello, Gemini. I want you to act as an expert in change management regarding data and AI. I am not a data and AI professional. My background is actually in history, and I went into the business world to work as a project manager. In my job, I am about to start using a new data and AI tool that is supposed to help me be more efficient and effective. This tool specializes in simplifying data and AI into visualizations. The problem is, I don't know anything about data and AI, so I don't know how to handle this new tool. What are things I can do to develop more confidence and skills to use this new tool? What are some foundational skills I may need in data and AI to use it? What are skills I can learn in data and AI literacy to empower me? Thank you for your help."

Prompt 2:

"My company is asking me to research ways to drive the adoption of a new data and AI tool. I have never been involved in a change management program for an organization, and this has been handed to me. I don't know where to begin. I am also not a data and AI professional by trade or background, so I am a little intimidated to help with a program with data and AI as a part of it. I want you to act as a powerful and innovative change management specialist whose sole purpose is to help me understand what change management is and how to deploy it in my organization. Please focus on helping me with how to communicate this change to get the organization excited about it, and how to deploy it for success. Thank you for your help with this."

Prompt 3:

"I have been hearing all the news around AI and it makes me nervous. I worry that AI may impact my career significantly. I don't know what to do. Please help me to understand ways I can build a mindset that is excited about data and AI and be more receptive to change. Include in the response key skills I can learn and books to read and study, so that I can evolve with the changes in data and AI that are going on around me."

Through change management, you can utilize a personal and/or organizational change framework. When using your own framework, learn from it, improve it if needed, and then utilize it in your career. You'll find that the prompt responses provide advice in a step-by-step, piece-by-piece structure. You don't need to do everything all at once.

For example, when I ran a prompt on Gemini, the response had three phases to it:

- **Phase 1—Understanding the "what" and the "why":** The "what" clearly shows me and/or the employees what the new product or program is, and what the change management process will be. The "why" matters because it helps people understand the reasons for implementing change.
- **Phase 2—Hands-on engagement and skill development:** Here you may see more of the "how" go into effect. How are we doing things now with the change, and what skills may we need to go forward? How can we develop these skills? You may also find hands-on skills and development that help make the change come to life for you.
- **Phase 3—Building confidence and trust:** Confidence and trust can be key for data and AI initiative change management. If people don't trust the data and/or AI, why would they use it? If you are looking to drive success in your organization, then make sure people have confidence and trust in you and the data and/or AI. This confidence can come from communicating effectively, which will be discussed below.

Within these phases, there were steps provided. Within Phase 1, Gemini recommended:

1. **Understanding the tool's purpose**—You should know what the purpose of a tool is if you are deploying one. Focus on why you are doing it, as well as what the specific tool does for the project.
2. **Find a mentor**—Do you have people in your career that you look up to that work in data and AI? Reach out to them and ask them to mentor you or be your buddy in data and AI. Now, you may ask: how

does a mentor help with change management? A mentor can help us to see things we weren't aware of previously. Maybe the mentor understands certain areas of the data and AI change better than us, or maybe the mentor helps us to understand the people that are affected most by the change. A mentor can potentially help us to understand and tackle the change better.

3 **Learn key terms**—Don't just march forward with a change management project without understanding the key terms. Ensure people have a good understanding of the terminology of the change. It could be that you create a dictionary for it and share this with your colleagues.
4 **Challenge assumptions**—Are there assumptions about the change that should be challenged? What assumptions may we need to address? One assumption we can make regarding change is that everyone understands what we are doing, i.e., what the change is. Another assumption we may make is that the person or team the change is for is excited or ready for the change. We should never assume they want the change or are ready for it. Finally, an assumption we can challenge is that those who may be using the data or AI have the skills to do so. We can't just stick things in front of people and assume they are ready to thrive with it. Of course, these aren't all the possible assumptions that could be challenged. Use your human and emotional intelligence to think of any assumptions you may make at times with those you work with.

Why Does Change Management Matter?

We have discussed change management, but does learning how to manage change and ensure people adopt it really matter? Remember New Year's Resolution Syndrome. You may have a desire to change, but desire doesn't guarantee the change will occur or take hold. We can't just hope and think it is going to happen.

Also, know that just because you have a change management program in your business, that doesn't mean people are going to adopt it. Just because the business buys a powerful tool or technology that will help the organization, that doesn't mean people will use it. In fact, in the data space, it has been the case that companies have bought good tools and technology only to have it fall flat.

One example of a new data or AI tool technology implemented where change went well is in my own career. When I entered an organization as a Senior Vice President of Data and AI transformation, I implemented literacy learning to help people with their skills. Then, over time, an "AI Champions" group was created where ideas were shared on how things are being used. That group was active in sharing what they were doing with others, or they issued challenges for people to take on. Finally, with one specific tool, I conducted a meeting for a group of people who could utilize the tool. This helped them to understand the tool more effectively. Knowledge can be power.

How many times in your career have you been told something is happening and you have to play along? Have you found it enjoyable to have to deploy something when you don't want to? How many times have you been told a new project or tool is coming but you didn't understand what it was, how to use it, and why it was being done? Now, imagine if your leadership had communicated better with you about everything happening and you were able to buy in, be a part of it. Doesn't that make more sense? No one likes getting emails saying you have new mandatory training. We should avoid making a change management program feel like this.

In the world of data and AI, your ability to understand why change management matters can help you have more confidence in the data and AI work to succeed. If you understand the change and how it impacts you, then you can develop the skills needed to help it thrive. You don't have to be playing guessing games; you are developing the skills that may help you to thrive with whatever change comes your way.

It also should be noted that you may not just thrive, but become a leader and advocate for the change and the work around it. This could maybe help you land new roles and/or a promotion in the organization. Change needs leaders and advocates. As you develop confidence and skills in data and AI, you can be a leader and advocate for the work around you.

Change Management Principles

Change management is about successful transformation bringing about innovation in an organization. A part of this is effective communication. Think about how you want to achieve organizational goals. Have you ever been told that something new is happening, but not why it is happening? When we are given a "why" and proper communication, it can be easier for buy-in to occur and easier for us to be on board with the change. The more people that are on board, the easier the transition from the change may be. Communication can be the secret sauce in data and analytics success. How can we communicate more effectively on data and AI change?

As mentioned above, change management should start with the "why" and be transparent and clear about the "what" and "how." Helping people to understand the "why," "what," and "how" can make it easier for them to take part in the change. If we don't know these things, we may become strong advocates against the change, even if it is the right thing we should be doing. It should also challenge assumptions, through open dialogue and feedback, and focus on upskilling and support, such as finding mentors within the business to act as buddies to those affected by the change.

One thing to note is that change management does not require a consensus among all participants, but communication should ensure that all employees understand why the change is taking place. If we are working toward total consensus, that can cause a headache or may be difficult to achieve. Instead, we need leaders and people to buy-in to the change and to invest time to help it drive forward successfully. One reason that consensus can be hard is we are human and have opinions. We like to have our ideas implemented. Some may be resistant to the change if we don't select their idea. So, we can work with people to hear from them and get them on board with the change.

There are ways to prompt AI to create an effective change management initiative. However, applying our human intelligence to change management is key. An IBM article highlights that successful change management means change is implemented throughout the company culture.[2] Remember our formula: with any data or AI initiative we must apply our human and emotional intelligence too.

People may fear change, so having good emotional intelligence can help leaders understand and manage their employees' feelings. I input the prompt into Gemini, asking about the key requirements for emotional intelligence when implementing change, and I received the following considerations:

1. self-awareness (your emotions)
2. self-regulation (managing your emotions)
3. empathy (understanding others' emotions)
4. social awareness (understanding the group dynamic)
5. relationship management (building trust and inspiring)

Ask yourself: where am I strong, and where could I improve?

CHANGE: LAYOFFS

Throughout my career I have had to utilize emotional intelligence during layoffs. I couldn't just jump in and start talking about big projects or a bonus I may receive. I had to read the room, understand people, have good social skills, be aware of what is happening, and make sure I am communicating well with all my co-workers. This includes those directly impacted, as well as those who were not. Those who weren't impacted by the layoffs could be friends with those who are. So, understanding how to communicate well with all is a good thing.

Personally, I have also been laid off, and having the skills to deal with it productively and without getting upset is important.

CHANGE: IMPLEMENTING DATA LITERACY

I have helped numerous organizations with data literacy. Counting all engagements, including speaking events and individuals attending from organizations, the number is high. In all of these instances, it was key for me to understand what individuals or organizations were already doing, the people who don't want the change, and the leaders who were not on board.

> What is interesting in my engagements with organizations is seeing the varying ways people react to the world of data literacy. I have found that some people buy in, understand the purpose, and want to either be more data literate themselves or have their organization move forward with it. Then, you will have those who are skeptical and don't want it. You will have organizations that invest in data literacy work and are buying in, and you will have organizations that talk the talk but don't walk the walk. However, guiding the skeptics through how they can implement this change can mean that many get on board.

Your Change Management Framework

Having your own personal change management framework can be impactful to help you deploy data and AI work effectively.

Step 1: Build Your "Why" and Understand the Change

For a change management program to work, you need to know your why and understand the change that is going to take place. So, make sure you build a why, and by understanding the change you can craft your message better, which, you will see, is the next step.

In your career, this doesn't only mean organizational changes. As you develop and work toward skills or promotions, you can understand your "why" and not just do things with guesswork or no understanding of why you are doing it. This also opens the door for you to be creative and curious. Your "why" doesn't have to be "learning this skill because I need to." It can be "learning this skill because I know it will help me accomplish X in my job," or "I am learning this skill so I can train my co-workers to also be successful here."

Step 2: Crafting the Message

When it comes to the change, you need to craft the communication and figure out how often you will communicate. Think of the stakeholders and those you need to get investment from; how should you communicate with them? Do you know how they like communications to come through?

If we are working on change for ourselves and managing it, we can also work toward communication and notes to ourselves on "why" we are doing it. This isn't necessarily crafting an email that is going to go out to others, unless you are using an accountability partner on your journey. Instead, we can write notes or in a journal for ourselves and thrive.

Step 3: Stakeholders and Buy-In

Work with the stakeholders, communicate with them and adjust as appropriate. Make sure you get true buy-in from those you need buy-in from. This may even include investment. Don't let them just say they agree with it, but get them to commit to the investment.

Step 4: POC—Deploying Change

Before doing a large deployment, do a smaller POC or POV (proof of concept or proof of value). Deploy this change and see how it goes: note which skills are needed to successfully deploy the change and how the change is received. Then, work with the participants to get the skills right. Use this pilot group to craft the POC and find what works and what you may need to do for the larger enterprise.

Now, you may ask who is in the pilot group? This can be determined with leaders and the work itself. If you are piloting marketing software, don't go to the finance team for all the participants. Instead, work with the marketing group. You can also work with those who you know may be enthusiastic for the change, as they can become cheerleaders for the work you are doing. Once the POC or POV is done, you can then start with crafting messages for the larger deployment so they understand it.

Step 5: Feedback Loop

Create a feedback mechanism for people to provide feedback on the change. This could be doing focus groups, a regular survey, or however it is easiest for you to receive feedback. Make sure you are open to all feedback. This could be for the small group and then, afterward, the large deployment.

If this is a personal change, you can find mentors or others to provide feedback to you. Just because it isn't done in a group doesn't mean you can't create feedback loops to empower you. You can even do this with generative AI and assess your skills or ask for feedback through the AI itself.

Step 6: Wide-Ranging Deployment

Now you should be ready for wide-ranging deployment. Set it in place, have communications, know what skills people may need to develop. Then, deploy. This may not be a quick process, but that is okay. Make sure you are vigilant in communication and helping people change.

Step 7: Monitor and Iterate

You need to continuously monitor the change and iterate where needed. Have flexibility. Have a feedback loop and allow changes to take place after the whole big project. You shouldn't just think people will change without continually monitoring it. It could be that you have great success with the initial rollout only to find it has fizzled away over time and the investment made for the change isn't bringing in the desired ROI.

Below are a couple of prompts for you to use to help you design your framework. However, do adapt these to make them more applicable to you. By developing frameworks you like, you will adopt them more effectively.

Prompt 1:

> "I am new to data and AI, but want to really succeed with it. I want to create an innovative change management framework that will help me to learn how to use data and AI to help me in my career. As AI is moving quickly, I want to make sure I am on top of it. Can you craft a personal data and AI change management framework which will help me be successful with data and AI?"

Prompt 2:

> "I am a junior member of my organization and we need to get working on AI success. The problem is that we are an organization that has a

long tradition of successful work and people are going to be hesitant to adopt a new way of doing things because of the success we have had. This doesn't mean we shouldn't do the change because we need to innovate for the future, but this concerns me. Can you help craft a data and AI change management program that helps communicate the 'why' to the organization, the benefits that come from AI, and please help me know how I can effectively contribute to this change management program? Thanks for your help."

> TIP
>
> Remember, when you are prompting, don't put sensitive data into the prompt unless it is protected and secure. We don't want to share confidential personal or company information.

Your Personal Data and AI Success Framework: Navigating the Future

To continue on your personal change journey to data and AI confidence, a framework is provided below.

Step 1: Pick Your Objective

For your own change management work, be clear and smart with our objective and know your "why" behind it. With your objective, align it to the business you work for, as well as your personal development and goals to ensure that your career progression course will be achievable. If you want to learn about data architecture, make that your objective. If you want to learn about generative AI or machine learning, make it that.

Step 2: Design Your Roadmap, Routine, and How You Will Be Consistent

Now that you know your objective, you will want to create a roadmap for it. You get to design your roadmap according your preferences and schedule. Ensure your roadmap enables you to work in time blocks and that you have milestones. You can also create your routine that will mean you are more likely to be consistent with it.

Step 3: Begin Your Roadmap and Celebrate Milestones

With your roadmap and routine in place, get going. As you go through your roadmap, ensure you are celebrating your milestones when you reach them. However, remember to be flexible with your work and pivot if necessary. Why would we want to pivot? It could be because you have found something different you need to work on or want to work on, or it could be because you realized you are taking on something that should be done later and you need a skill or training to help you get there. So, you can reset and design going forward.

Step 4: Apply Key Elements of Your Learning and Development

As you progress in the roadmap and milestones, ensure you are applying elements of your learning and development to your career. The world of data and AI has many theoretical elements, but for confidence and skills, you want to apply what you are doing. Practice and work through things. If you find you aren't completely ready on certain aspects, that's okay, because you can set it as a new objective.

Step 5: Document Your Progress and Create New Objectives As You Go

Finally, as you are going, document your journey along your roadmap. Through your journey, you may find new objectives you can take on. You may find new areas that interest you that you can explore. Document what went well and what didn't. Were there certain assessments you did that you received a high score on? Did you propose an idea about presenting data differently to your manager? Overall, documenting your data and AI journey is essential for tracking your progress.

Conclusion

Change management can empower you to data and AI success. Don't just suggest buying certain tools and technology or putting data in front of people. Instead, work to help people understand the change that these things may bring about, using your IQ and EQ too. Finally, data and AI change management is not just an organizational concept. Design and utilize your own personal success framework for data and AI to build your confidence to ultimately gain success.

KEY TAKEAWAYS

- Change matters and can be hard, so don't bite off more than you can chew.
- Utilize a change management framework to empower your change work.
- Utilize your personal data and AI success framework.

Notes

1 D. Miranda, C. Bottorff, and R. Watts. The Four Principles of Change Management, *Forbes*, August 7, 2022, www.forbes.com/advisor/business/principles-of-change-management/ (archived at https://perma.cc/TDP8-GBV3)

2 A. Iacoviello and A. Downie. What Is Change Management? IBM, www.ibm.com/think/topics/change-management (archived at https://perma.cc/JQ7S-4ZR7)

12

Your Mindset: Bringing It All Together

There is a lot of information on mindset, so this chapter aims to highlight its importance in relation to data and AI. Having the right mindset is a key part of helping us develop and evolve with the ever-changing data and AI landscape.

In this chapter, let's ensure you walk away with the right idea about mindset with data and AI. We will cover the following:

- What is mindset?
- Why does mindset matter to data and AI?
- How to develop your mindset, build your personal routine, and be consistent.
- Applying mindset to our formula Data + AI + IQ + EQ = Engineered Intelligence.

What Is Mindset?

Let's make sure we establish how we want to define mindset. Below are two definitions.

A world-renowned Stanford University psychologist, Carol Dweck, notes that there are two basic types of mindsets: fixed and growth.[1] We touched on these in Chapter 7; where someone with a fixed (or stagnant) mindset may believe they cannot improve their skills, someone with a growth mindset does, no matter how new they are to it.

Mindset is also defined as "a set of beliefs that shape how we make sense of the world and ourselves. It's like a mental attitude that affects how we interpret events and situations. It's not just about being positive or negative; it's a deeper framework that influences our thoughts, feelings, and behaviors."[2]

Therefore, our mindset is a powerful way we can move forward. Let's use an example from my life: ultra marathons. Why would one want to do ultra marathons? Well, to push limits. I have run multiple ultra marathons, and there are times you don't want to keep going but you do. I have a friend who has surpassed me in ultra marathons. At first, she didn't think she would finish a 28-mile race, and she has now completed three 100-milers at the time of writing. She clearly demonstrates a growth mindset where she keeps pushing forward.

Now, using the definitions above, let's define our data and AI mindset that we should adopt. Our data and AI mindset can be how we approach data and AI in our lives and how we achieve our own skills and confidence with them. It is our own personal lens through which to view data and AI.

Let's look at how you could prompt AI to create your own personal definition, and I will use myself as the example. I encourage you to do this. Why could it be important for you to create your own personal definition of mindset? Well, let me ask you this: is your mindset, the way you think, the way you approach things, the same as mine? The same as your colleague's or boss's? No, it isn't. Instead of trying to use the mindset that is defined for you, what if you create your own personalized definition and allow it to take you forward, to empower you? No one has the exact same mindset, as we are all shaped by different experiences and thoughts (a key part of our human intelligence!). So, create your own definition and be yourself; maybe you'll create the most powerful definition ever. Do it.

Prompt:

> "Hi, I love to learn. I work in data and AI. I am lucky enough to travel the world speaking on these topics. I want to ensure I have the right mindset to continue to develop and grow and move forward in this fast-paced data and AI world. I am married with five kids, I have written multiple books, I love the sport of rugby and coach it at the university

level. I write and journal. I love working out. With data and AI moving as fast as they are, I want to have the right definition of what mindset means and how I can apply it to me. Below, you will find two definitions of mindset. Please use these definitions and what you know about me to create a powerful definition of mindset that I can use going forward to ensure I have a place at the data and AI table. Thank you for the help."

Paste the definitions provided above into the prompt too, and then allow the AI to create your own definition.

So, with your new definition, let's look at how it can apply to data and AI and why it matters in these spaces.

Why Does Mindset Matter to Data and AI?

With data and AI, if it isn't a passion for you, if it isn't your background, if it isn't what you are looking to do every day of your career, then your mindset might be one of avoidance, one where you aren't wanting to even peek behind the curtain of these areas. You may fear the dystopian future or be concerned about job loss. That's not a bad thing, but what you do with these emotions matters.

If we have a growth mindset, we can attack things in the right way. Now, it is one thing to be motivated, and I hope you are, but it is a totally different thing to move forward in an intelligent manner and find your own personal success.

To begin with, if you aren't just naturally moving forward with the motivation to figure out how to use AI, is that a bad thing, or something you should worry about? No! For example, you may enjoy working out, but you aren't necessarily aiming to be a body builder. In the same way, you don't have to aspire to be a data and AI expert. You just need to adapt your mindset to one where you believe you have the ability to learn skills that enable confidence with data and AI. This positive, trusting mindset is the "how."

The "what" in a data and AI mindset is the task you are learning about or doing. There are many facets of data and AI: science, analysis, visualization, engineering, prompting, literacy.

Now, the "why" of mindset with data and AI may be the foundation of all success when it comes to our formula: Data + AI + IQ + EQ = Engineered Intelligence. We need to have our "whys." For me, my family is a big why in my life. I want to gain knowledge so I can be successful and provide for them. What is your "why" for learning and growing? Some of these could be:

- **To be part of a fast-moving industry:** Although some jobs may be impacted by AI, there are many emerging roles in the tech space. We can position ourselves to succeed with confidence and skills. Now, this won't necessarily be a positive for some who don't want to work in a fast-paced company. That is okay. Find your why and what works for you.
- **To harness the World Economic Forum skills:** Remember, in the top ten fastest growing skills, human skills made up 6 of the 10. The two top were "AI and big data" and "networks and cybersecurity." Then, the third was "technological literacy." We can call this data and AI literacy instead. Then, the fastest growing skills contained human-related skills in multiple places. Your "why" may be to develop skills in these spaces and be a part of those top ten fastest growing skills.
- **To get a better bonus:** Yes, utilizing data and AI may help propel us forward to more financial success within a company, especially if you are an integral part of the project. Does a larger bonus appeal to you? Maybe it isn't the bonus itself, but what you can do with it. Take the vacation you want, buy the car or house you want, invest for the future.
- **To be empowered in your goal setting:** Use data and AI to set better goals and move forward in your career. Can you utilize data and AI to achieve your goals and objectives, whether personal or career oriented? Yes, this is something you can do and it may help you to do them more effectively.

Overall, it is crucial to develop a mindset that enables us to succeed with data and AI. Use your own emotional intelligence and ask yourself: Do I have a fixed mindset and believe I can't learn data and AI?

Or do I have a growth mindset and believe I can do this? It is okay if you have a fixed mindset—recognizing this is the first step of your development. AI can help with this too; below is a prompt you can try.

> "I am worried I have a fixed mindset when it comes to learning data and AI. I don't know if I can do it. I am fearful I won't be able to learn fast enough or that it is too much for me. I want to have a growth mindset, but need to start small. Can you please help me understand steps I can take to develop and move forward with a growth mindset toward data and AI?"

The prompt response will provide ways to grow and develop your confidence and skills with a growth mindset.

How to Develop Your Mindset, Build Your Personal Routine, and Be Consistent

One key thing to think about is how to make small, incremental gains through your work. Having small wins can help you to progress. Let's help you see how to develop your mindset, then we can build a personal routine and be consistent with your development.

Steps to Developing Your Data and AI Mindset

I will give you a prompt again that you can use to identify how to grow and develop your mindset:
Prompt:

> "I am new to data and AI, and I really want to develop and grow my skills in this area. I feel like I am positioned well to do just that. I am eager and ready. My background is in writing. I am now looking to harness the power of data and AI to augment me, but I am fearful I won't be able to do it as well as I want. Can you please help me understand how to overcome this fear and develop a strong growth mindset for data and AI?"

Now, you should iterate this prompt to make it your own, using the three Cs—curiosity, creativity, and critical thinking—that we have

discussed throughout this book. To utilize creativity here, you could ask the prompt to give you ways that you can tie this data to stories which you are able to share with others. Here is an updated prompt that demonstrates how to iterate prompts more effectively:
Prompt:

> "I am new to data and AI, and I really want to develop and grow my skills in this area. I currently work as a high-school teacher, and I am eager and ready to learn. My background is in writing, and I enjoy it, but it can be time-consuming. I want to understand how to prompt AI well to create teaching notes from my slides and brainstorm helpful exercises for students. To help me do this, I want to utilize stories that high school students would understand and then share with the students
>
> "However, I am fearful I won't be able to do it as well as I want. I constantly have imposter syndrome, which can impact the way I come forward with confidence. Can you please help me understand how to overcome this fear and imposter syndrome, and develop a strong growth mindset for data and AI?"

Overall, I hope by now you are a bit eager to develop and grow within your own personal skill set and confidence. Don't forget, you matter, and your ideas, thoughts, and skills can be brought to the table. Some of the key elements to nurture a growth mindset when working with data and AI are as follows.

WILLINGNESS TO MAKE MISTAKES

In reality, as we develop with data and AI, we are going to make mistakes. Own it. Thrive from it. Run with it. If you feel right off the bat that you have to be perfect with data and AI, unfortunately, you may be setting yourself up to fail very, very quickly.

Instead, when we want to have the right mindset, we adopt Nelson Mandela's quote: "I never lose. I either win or learn."[3] You are now in a position to evolve with the right mindset for data and AI.

EAGERNESS TO LEARN

Hopefully, by this point in the book, you are eager to learn more and more. Developing is key. I personally am devoted to learning. I don't know everything about data and AI, not even close, but I have a hunger to learn. I read books regularly, listen to podcasts, and read articles and LinkedIn posts.

When we think about the right mindset when it comes to developing confidence and skills with data and AI, learning is fundamental to us. We need to be developing our data literacy: learning the skills to read, work with, analyze, and communicate with data. We also need to be developing our AI literacy: the ability to prompt, evaluate the prompt response, and then make decisions with the prompt.

Specific topics that we can study to further our confidence and skills with data and AI could be:

- learning how to build a stronger narrative around data and AI
- learning how to interpret the data better
- learning how to evaluate the prompt responses better
- learn how to make better decisions with data and AI outputs

Whatever you are learning, apply yourself to it and develop. You can truly learn how to grow and become more confident and skilled with data and AI.

NATURAL CURIOSITY

This goes along with eagerness to learn, but you should be asking questions all the time. Have the mindset like that of a child. Learn to formulate questions. Write them down. Input them as a prompt into AI to get answers. Don't lose out on the ability to ask questions regularly and miss out on the chance to grow because you don't ask it.

Willingness to make mistakes also aligns with natural curiosity. When you think about asking a question, do you ever get a pit in your stomach, feeling embarrassed to ask it? Do you fear what others may think? This is something you need to overcome. It's okay to ask the question that maybe no one else has. Most likely, someone else has that exact question and they don't want to ask it either.

THINK CRITICALLY

This one is big to me. Remember the three Cs of data literacy: curiosity, creativity, and critical thinking. These are things you can practice and strengthen without the need for technology to get started. You can ask questions, be creative, and critically think about everything! Don't weaken your cognitive muscles because you just want the data and AI to do it all.

Don't lose out on your emotional intelligence here, either. Critical thinking doesn't just need to be on technical things—we should ensure that we critically think about how our decisions with data and AI affect ourselves and others, with empathy. We want to work our cognitive muscles. In fact, not losing sight of what it means to critically think could result in better career opportunities. This closely ties in with asking questions—when you ask and determine the who, what, where, when, how, and why, you can make better decisions.

KNOW YOU CAN DEVELOP AND GROW

Ensure you have a belief in yourself. I hope that doesn't sound corny, but when it comes to fixed versus growth mindsets, the limiting belief that you can't do it, or you can't learn it, shouldn't be a part of the conversation for you. Know you have a seat at the data and AI table.

Your Framework for Routine and Consistency

We now have some principles around your mindset with data and AI. Before we conclude this chapter (and book) by discussing mindset in relation to each chapter of this book and our formula, let's give you some steps to setting up your routine and maintaining consistency whilst learning and developing your data and AI skills. The steps below are adapted from the Association for Talent Development's "7 Steps to Building and Sustaining a Lifelong Learning Routine."[4]

STEP 1: ESTABLISH LEARNING GOALS

To get started with your routine, step 1 is clearly establishing what your learning goal is. Don't be ambiguous. Set the goal, have the right mindset, and get going. Having clarity means that you can move forward with the ability to set a goal and know what you want to achieve.

STEP 2: UNDERSTAND YOUR LEARNING STYLE

Do you know your learning style? People can have various learnings styles: visual, auditory, reading/writing, kinaesthetic, or a mix of these. Do you like to read books? If the answer is yes, use that to your advantage. If you don't know your learning style, here is a prompt you can use to help determine it:

> "I want to learn what my learning style is. Can you craft an assessment and scoring system that will help me determine how I like to learn? Make sure you are clear, help me to understand the different learning styles, and please make the assessment 15 questions in length."

Learn in a style you enjoy, as this will give you a higher likelihood of success with your learning goals.

STEP 3: HAVE A VARIETY OF LEARNING METHODS

This ties in with step number 2. Make sure you include many ways to learn in your routine, from online courses to webinars and conferences. Ensure you also get a varied perspective on what you are learning. Don't just take things that confirm your beliefs off the bat (remember your critical thinking skills!) and instead learn from varying perspectives so you can learn as much as possible.

STEP 4: USE A LEARNING SCHEDULE

Create a learning schedule and then align with it. If you are busy, you may feel like you don't have time, but even 15 minutes can be beneficial.

You can prompt AI to help you find blocks of time for learning:

> "I want to build a learning schedule for me to use, but I just don't see how I can. My days are busy, I have kids practicing music in the morning before school, they go off to school and I go off to work. After school and work, we have chores, dinner, homework, practices. It just feels like too much. Can you help me find time in my day or help me create a planning schedule so I can be more consistent with my learning?"

Once you have your schedule, follow it as best you can.

STEP 5: GIVE MICROLEARNING A GO

This step coincides with a busy schedule. You do not need to learn about data and AI all at once. Instead, microlearn—as mentioned above, this could be 15 minutes a day. That seems much more manageable than trying to sit down for 4 hours. You are more likely to find it enjoyable and engaging too.

STEP 6: APPLY YOUR LEARNINGS

Did you ever ask in a math class "Where will I use this in the real world?" Well, with learning in data and AI, it can be helpful to take your learnings beyond the theoretical into the practical. Find use cases and applicability where you can use the data and AI you are learning about. Don't just read and not apply them. Can you imagine reading about weightlifting or running a marathon, doing nothing about it, and wondering why you aren't able to just run the marathon or lift like strong people? Put things into practice and apply learnings in your life. Don't be afraid of mistakes—mistakes are how you grow.

Consistency is the only effective way to achieve goals: like training for a marathon, if you run once every couple of weeks instead of running and training effectively daily, including days off for recovery, it will take longer. Similarly, when you are learning about data and AI, your consistent effort to apply learning can help you progress forward more than just reading about it. Don't miss out on the growth you can gain by consistently driving ahead.

STEP 7: MONITOR YOUR PROGRESS AND REWARD YOURSELF

Tracking your progress can be empowering to staying consistent. Why do you think this is so? If you aren't tracking, how will you know how far you have come? How can you visually see the progress? Tracking your progress can keep you honest with yourself and accountable. You can even go a step further and share your tracking with another who can be your accountability partner.

To help you with tracking, here is a prompt to help:

> "I am new to the data and AI space and really want to be a lifelong learner. I am just getting started, but I want to ensure I am tracking my progress. Can you suggest 10 innovative ways for me to track progress with my data and AI confidence and skills? I am a visual person, so a way to visually see progress would help. Thank you."

When I use this prompt, it helped me with the idea of using a "I Did This" jar. You can fill up a jar over time with wins, whether big or small. Then, you can take those wins out and read about your progress. Another creative way it gave me was to use visuals and color coding in a visual notebook that I jotted down my learnings in.

Then, as you progress, you can set milestones and have celebrations. Ensure you are celebrating your successes to avoid burnout.

Applying Mindset to Our Formula and the Chapters of This Book

Wow, here we are, the last section of the book. Can you believe you made it? How are you feeling about your data and AI skills right now? Are you gaining confidence? How is your mindset now, do you believe you can do this? Let us first go through the chapters and apply the mindset to each:

Chapter 1: The Formula for Success in the Age of Data and AI—This chapter outlined how you don't need to be an advanced data scientist or AI engineer to achieve success in the data and AI fields. You are more literate with data than you may realize and although AI can be a great partner to empower you in your life, remember our formula: Data + AI + IQ + EQ = Engineered Intelligence. This requires IQ and EQ, your human elements.

Chapter 2: What Does Data and AI Confidence Look Like?—Working on having a growth mindset in regard to data and AI will boost your confidence and ensure that you feel like you have a place at the data and AI table.

Chapter 3: Data Literacy: Your Journey Toward Success—Data literacy is the ability to read, work with, analyze, and communicate with data. Ensure you march forward confidently with a growth mindset, knowing you don't have to be a technical person, but you can apply data to decision making and empower yourself with more success.

Chapter 4: What Is AI and AI Literacy?—There are different forms of AI in the world, and you don't need to learn the full ins and outs of all of them. Like with data literacy, a growth mindset enables you to learn effectively and apply these learnings to your career.

Chapter 5: How to Build a Plan to Succeed with Data and AI—Having a growth mindset will help you to craft routines and learning schedules to improve your confidence and consistency when learning about data and AI.

Chapter 6: The Power of Data and AI Use Cases—AI is fun, it can be creative, but one thing you can focus on is to develop use cases that bring you value. If you are investing in data and AI, make sure you are receiving value in the end. You can't just buy tools and technology, and hope for success. Instead, plan for success by building out use cases. Maybe the use cases are as simple as AI being your personal chef or travel agent, or you have a more complicated use case. How can a growth mindset help with use cases? As we create use cases and try to find value in our AI work, we will inevitably have instances when a use case doesn't come to fruition or is something we need to adapt when it isn't going well. Without a growth mindset, this may knock our confidence, meaning we miss out and don't develop.

Chapter 7: Why Human and Emotional Intelligence Still Matter in the Age of Data and AI—Don't lose sight of your personal intelligence, both IQ and EQ. Your mindset should be that your personal intelligence matters. It doesn't mean it should supersede data and AI all the time, but your personal knowledge and skills can provide crucial context.

Chapter 8: Applying Your Human and Emotional Intelligence to Data and AI Decisions—As Chapter 7 discusses, IQ and EQ are hugely important. To apply them, you need to have a growth mindset—the belief that you can apply IQ and EQ to data and AI decisions.

Chapter 9: Talking the Language of Data and AI—A growth mindset helps you to learn new terminology and then confidently and effectively communicate with others about it.

Chapter 10: Build Better Value with Data and AI—Like use cases, value is something you may want to derive from data and AI. That value could be just new information or established goals. Whatever the value is that you are working toward, a growth mindset helps you apply yourself to it.

Chapter 11: Becoming a Data and AI Leader in Your Organization: The Power of Change Management—Change isn't always easy. So, we can have a mindset to step into a more leadership-style role to help people to move forward. AI can be full of hype and fear, and so we want to ensure that we develop use cases and value, to encourage others in our organization to properly adjust and evolve.

Our Formula and Mindset

To wrap up our book, let's discuss mindset in relation to our formula introduced to us at the very beginning of the book:

Data + AI + IQ +EQ = Engineered Intelligence

- Data—We don't have to be data scientists in order to develop skills to succeed with data.
- AI—A growth mindset can overcome the buzz, hype, and negative news surrounding AI. With confidence in our ever-growing skills, we can sit at the AI table.
- IQ—Our human intelligence matters in this technology driven world. We have ideas, thoughts, and experience that can be augmented by data and AI. We can partner with data and AI, apply our knowledge to it, and make better decisions.
- EQ—Our emotional intelligence is a crucial part of what we do with data and AI and is intrinsically linked with mindset: we can be self-aware of where we are with our skills and abilities. We can also help people to succeed with data and AI, to help them not fear what's happening and to lead people in these spaces.
- Engineered Intelligence—The combination of the data/AI and the human. Don't leave yourself out.

Don't forget, in this age of AI, the human matters. Your ideas, thoughts, and creativity can be combined with, and augmented by, data and AI. Now that you are done with the book, go out and develop confidence to succeed with data and AI.

Conclusion

Well, here we are at the end of this book. How are you feeling? Do you feel more confident, that you have a place at the table? Did you learn something new that you can take forward? Were you inspired to write something down? What are you going to take from this book? How are you going to use it to propel you in your career?

We have covered some key skills that you can think about and maybe work with, with data and AI. The three Cs of data literacy we can perhaps now call the three Cs of data and AI literacy. We also have the three Is (information, insight, and intelligence) and they can be important concepts to build your confidence. We have also discussed the significance of using your personal data points (IQ) and your emotional intelligence (EQ) as part of your formula for success.

This book can be a starting point, a beginning for you. It doesn't hold every single possible topic or answer there is, but it can help you develop skills. Nobody should fear data and AI; understand that you have a place at the table. I hope this book has helped you feel that you can build and develop on your journey to data and AI skills and confidence—good luck!

KEY TAKEAWAYS

- Create your own personal definition of mindset and apply it.
- Don't pattern your mindset after everyone else's, and work on having a growth mindset.
- Our formula is Data + AI + IQ + EQ = Engineered Intelligence.

Notes

1 Farnam Street. Carol Dweck: A Summary of Growth and Fixed Mindsets, fs. blog /carol- dweck -mindset/ (archived at https://perma.cc/T6NK-5JF4)

2 J. Tosini. What Is a Mindset? Mindset, June 20, 2025, mindsetonline.com/what-is-a-mindset/ (archived at https://perma.cc/3T33-GLJH)

3 A. Herron. Remembering Nelson Mandela: "I Never Lose. I Either Win or Learn," *Indianopolis Recorder*, July 15, 2021, indianapolisrecorder.com/remembering-nelson-mandela-i-never-lose-i-either-win-or-learn (archived at https://perma.cc/N75Z-X5WG)

4 B. Gooding. 7 Steps to Building and Sustaining a Lifelong Learning Routine, ATD, October 8, 2024, www.td.org/content/atd-blog/7-steps-to-building-and-sustaining-a-lifelong-learning-routine (archived at https://perma.cc/L2NF-DNHP)

INDEX

The index is filed in alphabetical, word-by-word order. Acronyms and 'Mc' are filed as presented; numbers are filed as spelt out in full. Locators in italics denote information within figures.

Looking for another book?

Explore our award-winning books from global business experts in Business Strategy

Scan the code to browse

www.koganpage.com/business-strategy

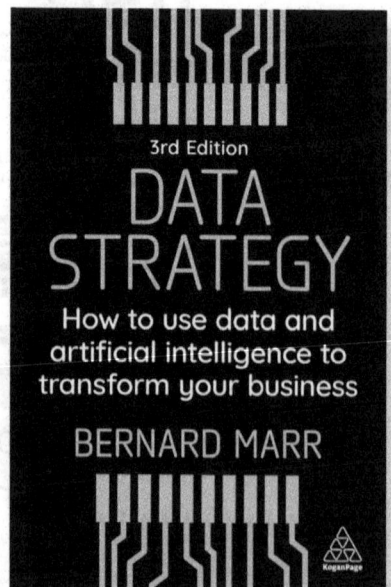

From 4 December 2025 the EU Responsible Person (GPSR) is:
eucomply oÜ, Pärnu mnt. 139b – 14, 11317 Tallinn, Estonia
www.eucompliancepartner.com

www.ingramcontent.com/pod-product-compliance
Lightning Source LLC
Chambersburg PA
CBHW071554210326
41597CB00019B/3242